Joy
of Wushu
歡喜武術

Author and Photographer Lily Liu Chung
Co-Author Melody Chung
Visual Designer Jessica Liu Brookshire

Think Big Publishing

Inspired by

the beauty and sophistication of Wushu,
Lily Liu Chung and Jessica Liu Brookshire
collaborate to form this unique project.

 Published by Think Big Publishing

ISBN: 0-9774063-0-X
Website: www.joyofwushu.com
email: info@joyofwushu.com
FAX: 1-408-257-5547

國際標準圖書編號: 0-9774063-0-X
網站: www.joyofwushu.com
電子信箱: info@joyofwushu.com
傳真: 1-408-257-5547

Author and Photographer Lily Liu Chung
Co-Author Melody Chung
Visual Designer Jessica Liu Brookshire
Book Cover Designed by Jessica Liu Brookshire

作者與攝影:劉曉莉
共同作者:鍾珮璇
視覺設計:劉玉寧
封面設計:劉玉寧

歡喜武術

Calligraphy by Au Ho-Nien
國畫大師歐豪年題字

III

Contents

目錄

I would like to dedicate this book to my loving parents, my brothers Bill and Bruce, my husband Alan and my three precious children: Eric, Melody and Katie. You all are the sunshine of my life.

謹將此書獻給我最親愛的爸媽、哥哥曉驊、弟弟哮虎、先生嘉光，與三個心愛的孩子：偉盛、珮璇、媛媛。你們是我生活的動力與快樂的泉源。

Lily Liu Chung
劉曉莉

I would like to dedicate this book to my loving parents, who never stop encouraging and supporting me.

Also to my beloved husband Scott, who brightens and colors my canvas of life with his enduring love.

And lastly to my cousin Lily, for giving me this amazing book project opportunity and inspiring me with her exceptional energy and passion for Wushu.

謹將此書獻給我親愛的父母，
他們從未停止鼓勵我、支持我；
也獻給我所摯愛的丈夫史考特，
他以無盡的愛豐富了我的人生畫布；
最後，感謝我的表姐曉莉，以她超然的精力與
對武術的熱情，鼓舞我參與本書的製作。

Jessica Liu Brookshire
劉玉寧

Acknowledgments
致 謝

We would like to thank all the sifus, coaches and students who contributed to this project. In addition, we would like to acknowledge the following individuals who kindly offered their time and knowledge to help us to accomplish this book.

本書能順利完成，除了感謝所有接受訪問的師父、教練與學生外，
要特別感謝以下長輩與朋友在各方面的鼓勵、支持與協助。

Gigi Oh	簡琪
Grandmaster Dao Yun Chen	陳道雲老師
Grandmaster Pui Chan	陳培師父
Venerable Shi Quolin	釋果林師父
Grandmaster Jin-Sheng Tu	涂金盛師父
Master Patti Li	郝致華教練
Coach Li Jing	李靜教練
Coach Phillip Wong	菲利普‧黃教練
Coach Zhang Hong Mei	張宏梅教練
Master Tony Chen	陳朝輝師父
Master Fei Chen	陳飛師父
Coach Brent Hamby	漢比教練
Master Shu Dong Li	李書東教練
Gwong Yih Lee and Angela Lee	李廣益、鄭時寧
Ernie Lee and Fay Lee	李爾尼、李費
Au Ho-Nien	歐豪年
Dr. Hsing Kung	龔行憲博士
Jentai Tsai	蔡仁泰
Howard Lee	李厚維
Ginny Soong	宋晶宜
Mary Carson	瑪麗‧卡爾森
Scott Brookshire	史考特‧布魯克夏爾
Sheng D. Chiu	邱勝典
David Yu	游輝弘
Phillip Pai	白立品
Han-lin Peng	黃韓玲
Maria Chen	唐夢君
Maggie Li	李喬琚
Barbara Monroe	芭芭拉‧夢露
Daniel Brookshire	丹尼爾‧布魯克夏爾
Michelle Wu	吳佩真
Karen Quach	凱倫‧夸格

Author's Note

In December 2002, I introduced my daughter Melody to Chinese martial arts. Thoroughly convinced that the aesthetic yet challenging art would benefit her physically, I had also hoped that she would acquire a deeper understanding of her Chinese roots.

Her first practice, however, ended in a miserable feeling: while the other students pressed their temples against their knees, leapt across the mats, and practiced full sets, Melody struggled with basic kicks and stances. Not only was she deeply intimidated, but she also refused to go back. I told her, however, that I had already paid the month's tuition, and so I encouraged her to try a few more times before giving up.

Thank goodness she did, because her first-glance failure blossomed into a blessing. Three months after her first encounter with Wushu, she told me, "Mom, thank you for giving me the best gift in my whole life." Aside from developing a passion for Wushu, Melody has more endurance, better time management skills, and a pride in her life. Wushu has truly become the love and source of happiness for both of us.

Like other parents, I am a "voluntary chauffeur." Even after two years, I still enjoy watching my daughter train. I am always touched by the interaction between the coach and students, the training that the students endure, and of course the power of Wushu. The martial art truly challenges a person's potential, patience, and endurance. Whenever I have the chance, I always recommend other children to begin learning Wushu. As time wore on, I started to practice Taiji myself. I came to a startling realization: I wanted to write a book about Wushu. Driven by motivation and gut, I collected and organized information, snapped photographs, and conducted interviews. The goal of the project was to use a modern way to portray the beauty and spirit of Wushu, so as to attract and educate the community.

In July 2003, I visited Boston with Melody's teacher, Grandmaster Dao Yun Chen. There, I met and interviewed Wah Lum Kungfu Sifu Pui Chan, the founder of over 30 branches of the Wah Lum Kungfu system! What's more, approximately 90% of the students weren't of Asian descent. I was amazingly touched by the fact that they were so sincere and respectful towards Chinese martial arts. The students truly believed in the motto, "Respect ancestors, respect the teacher, respect the teaching, learn the kindness, learn the art, and learn Kungfu." I felt they were more Chinese than Chinese!

Since that time, I have encountered over a hundred of coaches and students, spanning from the east coast to the west coast. Although these coaches and athletes may differ in age, gender, ethnicity, and religion, everyone shares the same passion and is so hopelessly in love with Wushu. This passion reinforces my opinion that Chinese martial arts is a wonderful subject to work on.

Working on the project, however, was not a simple task. The difficulties surpassed my imagination; with such a broad topic, it was arduous to edit and select from thousands of photos, write a bilingual manuscript, and contact dozens of people. Although I often spent my holidays and nights working on the project, I enjoyed the entire process. With the tremendous contributions of my cousin Jessica and daughter Melody, we made the mission possible.

Joy of Wushu project took us over three years to accomplish. We hope that readers will cherish the opportunity to learn more about Wushu from our efforts. Wushu is a deep art and has become so popular throughout the world. There's a Chinese saying that goes, "Your sifu introduces you to the art, but it depends on your own effort to make it work." It truly depends on an individual's effort and consistency to succeed in life. Bless everyone: happily practice Kungfu and enjoy Wushu learning.

Lily Liu Chung

緣 起

2002年12月，送女兒珮璇去學武術，一方面是認為習武可以強身健體，一方面可以增強孩子對中國文化的認同感。

不過，第一次珮璇去上武術課，看到班上同學都能做高空跳躍或輕易劈腿，心生畏懼，找足藉口不願再回去，我心生一計，對她說：「媽咪已經付了學費，妳至少還得試幾次看看。」她這才硬著頭皮回去上課。才訓練了二、三個月，孩子的態度卻完全轉變，當時才剛過十三歲生日的她，語重心長地告訴我：「媽媽，這是一生中，您送給我最好的禮物！」她似乎比以前更能吃苦、更有耐性，做事變得很有計畫；我不清楚這樣的影響是如何形成的，但奇妙的是，之後，武術同時成為我們母女倆生活的一部分重心與快樂的泉源！

長期接送孩子上課，我經常靜靜地盤坐在武館角落，觀察課堂中師生的互動，教練努力教學而嘶聲力竭，學生專注學習而汗流浹背，我除了深受感動，也體會武術帶給習武者的影響真是巨大的，武術是一種挑戰人體能量極限的運動，可以訓練一個人堅毅不拔、沉著穩定。我一有機會碰到舊雨新知，都會極力推薦他們的孩子學武術，一陣子後，我自己也開始練起太極拳，並在腦中策畫《歡喜武術》的創作，一邊搜集資料，一邊進行拍照，希望用一種較現代化的手法，呈現武術的力與美和文化內涵，來吸引一般人的興趣，也讓更多的人受益。

2003年7月，在武術名家陳道雲老師的引介下，我在波士頓訪問了開設三十多個武術分館的美國華林功夫陳培師父，發現數千名習武的學生有百分之九十以上都是非華人，而且以美國白人居多。我非常驚訝，有那麼多美國人對功夫與武術充滿興趣。最打動我的是，這些美國人用很虔誠、尊敬的心習武，並對中國功夫老祖宗的教導「尊祖、尊師、尊教導，學仁、學藝、學功夫」身體力行，對中國文化的珍惜，比中國人有過之而無不及！

進行訪問期間，我先後在美國東西兩岸接觸與訪問了上百名習武的師父、教練與學生，發現他們對武術的執著與著迷，已到了「不可自拔」的地步，因此讓我更加堅信與興奮，武術是魅力無窮的運動與藝術，是一個絕佳的寫作題材。不過，寫《歡喜武術》這本書，難度大大超越我的想像，武術的範疇實在太大了，我既非受過攝影專業訓練，更非武術專家，再加上用中英文寫作，要克服與面對的技術性難題就是一大串，光是在坐在電腦前處理數萬多張的數據照片，就是一項艱巨的工程。雖然經常犧牲睡眠與假日，卻是在歡喜愉悅的心情下，進行這本書的創作。

這本書的完成，除了表妹劉玉寧是一大功臣，女兒珮璇也出了不少的力。玉寧表妹自幼在藝術上有天份，能把原本看起來很普通的一張照片，運用電腦動畫科技與自身特殊的品味，化成賞心悅目、百看不厭的攝影藝術品；而這本書也在她的精心設計下，得以清新脫俗地呈現在讀者面前。女兒珮璇則幫著我一起搜集、消化資料、一同訪問名師，兩人對每一段文字、每一個章節的寫作與整理，都做了詳細的討論。一路走來，母女感情加深，兩人之間突然增加了許多共同的話題，這個額外的收穫，還要拜武術之賜呢！

《歡喜武術》前後歷時三年終於問世，希望透過我們的觀察、訪問、創作、整理與努力，讓大家對中國武術的魅力與陽剛之美，能有另類的認識。武術是一門人人可以窺其堂奧的藝術，在全球已形成了一股盛行的浪潮，武館像雨後春筍，一個接一個在各地萌芽生根，習武的人也越來越多，中國人說：「師父領進門、修行在個人」，要領略其中的精萃，還是要靠個人的努力與堅持，在此謹祝福大家：開開心心練功夫、歡歡喜喜學武術！

劉曉莉

Joy
of Wushu

第一部
Part I

Introduction to Wushu
武術概略

What is Wushu?
何謂武術?

In many ways, Wushu represents the soul of China. Deeply rooted in spirituality and philosophy, Wushu is a term used to classify all Chinese martial arts styles under one name. Literally translated, "wu" means military and "shu" means art or skill. Wushu therefore means Chinese martial arts.

The Chinese character that represents wu is composed of two parts. The first part, "止" means "to stop." The second, "戈" is a pictograph of a spear. When combined, the term symbolizes the idea of using military power to subdue violent disorder. By promoting peace, Chinese martial arts serve and protect while avoiding conflict.

Wushu is a national sport in China, much as Tae Kwon Do is for Korea, football for the United States, or soccer for Brazil. The most popular sport in a country of over 1.3 billion people, Wushu is practiced in nearly every province of China.

從各方面來說,武術是中國的國魂,博大精深。武術一辭,概括所有中國各家門派的武藝。以字面解釋,「武」代表軍事,「術」代表藝術或技能,所以武術意指中國的武學藝術。

中國文字中的「武」字,由兩個部分組成。第一部分──止,意思是阻止,第二部分──戈,是槍的形象文;合而為一,象徵以武力征服暴力動亂。為倡導和平,中國武術在進行保衛的同時,也用來避免衝突。

武術是中國的國家運動,如同韓國的跆拳道、美式足球、巴西的足球。在1.3兆人口的中國,每個省份都有武術運動。

Jeffrey Basilio Pagtalunan
Opposite: **Jeffrey Lee, Jennifer Haight and Cheri Haight**

Contemporary Wushu and Traditional Kungfu

Chinese Wushu can be categorized into two main groups: Contemporary Wushu and Traditional Kungfu. The first, which focuses on training and competing, is a highly gymnastic, technical demonstration sport that emphasizes complexity of movements, higher jumps and visual expression. Key elements include speed, flexibility, balance, coordination and presentation.

In contrast, Traditional Kungfu broadly encompasses the ancient fighting practice. The application-based fighting of Kungfu emphasizes techniques of style, physical conditioning, the relationship between internal and external power, and the healing tradition. Kungfu is characterized by several styles, such as Shaolin, Wudang, Omei and hundreds more.

Although Wushu has been with the Chinese for well over 1,500 years, only recently has it spread to other countries. In the last few decades, the captivating art has increasingly become more popular throughout the world, with over 97 nations participating in the International Wushu Federation (IWUF). Moreover, the sport was inducted as an official medal event in the Asian Games in 1991. As the sport steadily expands its global presence, people across the world are gradually discovering and appreciating the art of Wushu.

Cheri Haight
薛莉 · 海德

4

現代武術與傳統功夫

中國武術可以分成兩大類：現代武術與傳統功夫。現代武術著重訓練與比賽，是一種要求高度體能與技術的運動，強調動作難度、彈跳高度、視覺表現；要點包括：速度、柔軔性、平衡、協調與整體表現。

相對比較，傳統功夫比較廣泛，包含了自古以來的打鬥方式。以實用為主的功夫，強調招式技巧、體能狀態、內外調和與傳統的醫療。功夫門派眾多，包括少林、武當、峨嵋等百多家。

盡管武術在中國已有一千五百多年的歷史，但直到最近，才流傳到其他國家。在過去幾十年間，魅力無窮的武術越來越受到歡迎，現在全球已有97個國家是國際武聯的成員；此外，武術運動於1991年也正式成為亞洲運動會的比賽項目。武術運動在全球各地穩定擴展，人們也漸漸體悟與欣賞武術這門藝術。

Jeffrey Lee
李明道

5

Definition of Kungfu
功夫的定義

"Kungfu" does not actually translate into "Chinese martial arts." Instead, it literally means "skill from highly concentrated effort," or simply "hard work." Used as a general term in the Chinese language, Kungfu therefore means the mastery of any art. Consequently, an accomplished writer or a competent chef can have "good Kungfu."

An alternative definition of Kungfu is "a disciplined person," with "kung" meaning discipline and "fu" meaning person. By executing martial art techniques, students become disciplined through repetition, practice and concentration. Although Kungfu is multi-faceted, the ultimate goal is to strive for a harmonious blending of the body, mind and spirit.

With the popularity of Hong Kong Films, Bruce Lee and *Kung Fu*–the television series, the unknown term "Wushu" became familiar to the mainstream English community in the 1960s. Before that, the term was primarily referred to as "Chinese boxing."

Left to right: **Vara Reese, Melody Chung, Jeffrey Lee, Sifu Shi Quolin and Shi Xiao Long**

一般人所稱的「功夫」，直譯並非武術，它可以被解釋為「高度集中努力下獲得的技能」，簡單地說，就是「努力工作」。在中國語言中，功夫是一個廣義的名詞，代表對任何技術的掌握。所以，一位有成就的作家或能幹的廚師，可以稱他們有「好功夫」。

還有一種解釋，功夫代表「有紀律的人」，「功」代表紀律，「夫」指的是人，在練習武術技能時，學生經由反覆練習與集中精神來達到自律。雖然功夫是多面性的，但最終目標則是達到身心靈的和諧。

西方英語系國家對功夫並不熟悉，直到1960年代，經由李小龍主演的香港電影與《功夫》電視影集，功夫才盛行起來。在此之前，功夫被解釋做「中國拳擊」。

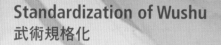

Standardization of Wushu
武術規格化

In order to create a universal standard, Wushu was modernized by the People's Republic of China in 1949. Masters and coaches across China gathered to produce compulsory movements for the competition floor.

Today's routines (taolu) are no longer compulsory and instead, are tailored toward individual strengths. Routines include long fist, southern fist, broadsword, straightsword, spear, staff/cudgel, Taiji and southern broadsword.

為了制定一個全面性的標準，中國政府於1949年將武術標準化，來自全國各地的武師與教練相聚在一起，討論出比賽場上各項規定的基本動作與套路。

目前國際間的比賽已不採用標準套路，依個人特色的自選套路。規定的套路包括：長拳、南拳、刀、劍、槍、棍、太極、南刀。

Sifu Tony Chen
陳朝輝師父

Sifu Fei Chen
陳飛師父

Differences Between Wushu and Other Martial Arts
武術與其他武藝的差別

NAME 名稱	ORIGIN 發源地	TRANSLATION 翻譯	BRIEF DESCRIPTION 簡要說明
Wushu 武術	China 中國	War arts 軍事技術	A general term for Chinese martial arts 中國武藝的通稱
Tae Kwon Do 跆拳道	Korea 韓國	Way of hands and feet 手腳的方法	Primary form of Korean unarmed combat 韓國主要的非武器競技
Karate 空手道	Japan 日本	Empty hand 空手	All parts of the anatomy used to punch, strike, kick or block 利用身體各部位出拳、打、踢或阻擋
Aikido 合氣道	Japan 日本	Way of spiritual harmony 心靈和諧的方法	Based on aikijutsu, non-aggressive self-defense, harmony and grace of movement 源自合氣柔術，非功擊性的自我防衛，動作和諧與優雅
Judo 柔道	Japan 日本	Gentle way 溫和的方法	Art of self-defense similar to wrestling, adapted from jujitsu 與摔角類似的自我防衛法，從柔術演變而來

Benefits of Wushu
習武的益處

There are numerous benefits to practicing Wushu. Practitioners both young and old can experience the physical, emotional, mental, social and spiritual benefits of this lifelong art. Wushu strengthens the body, improves flexibility, toughens the mind and rejuvenates the spirit.

According to Sifu Thomas Haase of Wah Lum Kung Fu of Tampa in Florida, people benefit from their training in more ways they can imagine. "Many benefits are subtle changes or shifts in your personality and viewpoints," he says. "These gradual changes slowly begin to alter your outlook and attitude towards life and the people in it. That is why Kungfu is a lifelong art. The longer you practice, the further you grow and the more you realize how little you have learned."

習武有許多好處，無論是年輕或年長的人，都能透過這個可以終身學習的藝術，在身體、情緒、精神、社交與心靈上獲得益處。武術能增強體能、增加柔韌度、強化心理、活化心靈。

根據佛羅里達州Tampa華林功夫師父唐夏士表示，一般人自武術訓練中所得到的益處，比他們想像中要來得大。「許多益處包括個性上與看法上的微妙轉變。」他說：「這些逐漸的改變，會慢慢地開始轉換你的個性與看法。武術是一種終身學習的藝術，學習的時間愈久，愈能成長，你也能更加體會自己的不足。」

Grandmaster Dao Yun Chen
陳道雲教練

Matt Berberi
邁特・布伯瑞

Challenges
挑戰

"Wushu challenges me to execute more difficult movements and combinations.
I'm always trying to be perfect, and that just makes it endlessly fun."
– Alvin Hsing, College school student

「武術挑戰我去嚐試更高難度的動作與組合，我常試著去表現得更完美，也就是因為如此，武術的樂趣無窮無盡。」
— 邢思作，大學生

Confidence
自信

"Because of Wushu, I now have the spirit to go on stage and perform."
– Jenny Tu, middle school student

「因為習武的關係，我現在終於有勇氣站在台前表演。」
— 涂晏維，國中生

Deanne Chen
陳迪安

Fitness
健康

"Wushu made me more athletic and durable. After I started learning, my Physical Education grades went up!"
– Deanne Chen, high school student

「武術讓我更強壯與增進耐力，在我習武後，我的體育成績進步了。」
— 陳迪安，高中生

Focus
集中力

"I've learned how to control my mind and body from Wushu training. Every time I train, I clear my mind so that I can do my best."
– Christopher Chua Quiambao, high school student

「我從武術訓練當中學會如何控制自己的身心，每次訓練，我會靜下心，好讓自己全力以赴。」
— 坤寶，高中生

Jeffrey Lee
李明道

Goals
目標

"Asides from being more disciplined, Wushu has helped me to focus on my goals, whether they are short or long-term."
– Adam Chun, college student

「除了更加自律外，武術幫助我清楚地設定目標，無論短程或長程。」
— 鍾亞當，大學生

Humility
謙虛

"Wushu has made me humble—no matter how good I may be, there will always be someone better."
– Jeffrey Lee, high school student

「武術讓我更加謙虛 — 不管自己有多好，總有人比我更棒。」
— 李明道，高中生

Making Friends
結交朋友

"Chinese martial arts are an escape from the busy hustle and bustle of life. I have made many friends and met many people."
– Jason Jenkins, computer engineer

「武術讓我暫時忘卻每天生活的煩瑣，我交到很多朋有，與認識了很多人。」
— 詹肯斯，電腦工程師

Relaxation
鬆馳

"Wushu keeps the stressful things out of my mind and allows me to feel more relaxed."
– Chris Wang, college student

「武術能驅趕我的壓力，讓我覺得更加鬆馳緊張。」
— 王如恩，大學生

Jack Tu
涂聖成

Teamwork
團隊合作

"Wushu has changed my approach to physical fitness and has taught me more about teamwork."

– Jeffrey Basilio Pagtalunan, college student

「武術改變我的體能狀態，並且讓我學到團隊合作。」

—— 派格塔魯南，大學生

Jeffrey Basilio Pagtalunan
派格塔魯南

Wushu Classifications
武術分類

Wushu can be classified using one of three methods:
1. Northern and Southern
2. Shaolin, Wudang, Omei and Others
3. Internal and External

武術可以用三種方法分類：
1. 北拳與南拳
2. 少林、武當、峨嵋與其他門派
3. 內家拳與外家拳

● **Wudang**
武當

● **Shaolin**
少林

● **Omei**
峨嵋

Northern and Southern
北拳與南拳

Wushu styles can be divided into two categories: Northern or Southern, depending on which side of the Yangtze River it originated. Northern styles therefore originate from the upper half of Mainland China. These styles tend to emphasize expressive techniques, acrobatic tricks and open movements. Hollywood star Jet Li constantly executes Northern styles in his movies.

On the other hand, Southern styles originate from the bottom half of Mainland China. These styles tend to focus on strength and power, with a stress on firm stances and strong hand techniques. Jackie Chan and the late Bruce Lee often used Southern styles.

武術的形式還可分成北拳與南拳兩大類，以揚子江做為分界。北拳源自中國北方，較強調表現的技巧、特技與開放式的動作，好萊塢明星李連杰經常在電影中表現北拳的武打招式。

南拳源自中國南方，強調爆發力、站功與手型技巧，成龍與李小龍通常表現的是南拳的招式。

Shaolin, Wudang, Omei and Other Styles
少林、武當、峨嵋與其他門派

Shaolin, Wudang and Omei are just three of the many styles of Chinese Wushu. Shaolin is the most popular style and is generally said to originate from a form of fighting practiced at Shaolin Temple in Henan province. Wudang is the name of a mountain used by Daoists in Hebei province, and Omei is a major Buddhist mountain in Sichuan province. There are also other famous styles such as Taiji, Bagua.

少林、武當、峨嵋，是中國武術的三大門派。少林源自河南省少林寺，是少林寺發展出的特別武學；武當源自河北的武當山，道家的發源地；峨嵋則源自四川峨嵋，佛教聖地。其他著名門派還包括太極、八卦等。

Wudang Grandmaster
Zhong Yun Long
武當鍾雲龍大師

Master Patti Li
郝致華教練

Internal and External
內家拳與外家拳

Internal (soft) styles promote health, enhance longevity and improve vitality. Practitioners control their internal organs and flow of internal energy, and strength tends to come from the torso and legs. Examples of internal styles include Taiji, Bagua (Eight Trigram Palm) and Mind Shape Fist.

External (hard) styles build physical attributes by using muscular and physical strength. Practitioners condition the external parts of their body by using specific arm and leg muscles. External styles, like Contemporary Wushu, are usually more appealing to younger practitioners.

內家拳主要目的在促進身體健康、延年益壽、增進活力。練習者可以控制其內在器官與內在能量的流量,力量來自於軀幹與腿部,例如太極、八卦掌與形意拳。

外家拳利用肌肉與身體的力量來建立外在的力度,學習者利用特殊手腳的肌肉力量進行練習。例如現代武術較重視外在表現,對年輕人較具吸引力。

Opposite:
Grandmaster Dao Yun Chen
陳道雲教練

Charles Shao Hwang
黃孝傳

Usage Note
用法註解

When Chinese words are translated into English, some translators use Mandarin sounds while others use Cantonese sounds. These differences in capitalization, spelling, spacing and apostrophes can often lead to confusion. In this book, we use the Pinyin versions of these Chinese terms. The exceptions are our usage of Kungfu and Sifu, which are more widely recognized. The following table includes a list of other common terms, but please note that similar spellings mean the same thing.

中文翻譯成英文時，有些人採取國語 (普通話) 的翻譯方法，有些人則採用廣東話發音。這些在大小寫、拼法與間距方面都造成差異，有時加上所有格符號後，更令人混淆。本書使用的是拼音法，但 Kungfu 與 Sifu 除外，因為已經被普遍使用。下面的表格，說明本書採用的英文術語，另外列明其他相通的用法。

TERMS USED IN THIS MANUSCRIPT 本書使用的英文術語	OTHER COMMON TERMS 其他用法
Kungfu 功夫	Kung Fu, kung-fu, Gong Fu, Kuo shu (國術)
Wushu 武術	Wu Shu, Wusu
Sifu 師父	Shi-Fu, Shifu
Taiji 太極	Tai Chi, T'ai Chi, Taiji Quan, Tai Ji, Taijiquan
Qigong 氣功	Chi Kung, Chi Kong, Qui Kung, Qi Gong
Omei 峨嵋	Ermei, Emai, O-mei

Collin Lee 李佳龍

"Wushu has made me much stronger than anyone my normal size and age. "
— *Collin Lee*

「武術讓我在同年齡的朋友當中，更具柔韌性與壯碩。」
— 李佳龍

Personal Reflections 個人感言

Date of Birth: October 31,1989
Bentley Middle School, California
• 2005 U.S. Wushu Team Member
• 2002-2004 United States Chinese Kuoshu Federation—Teen Male Competitor of the Year
• 2003 Youth Overall International Champion—Sao Paulo-Brasil TWKF

生日：1989年10月31日
加州賓特利中學學生
• 2005年美國國家武術隊隊員
• 2002-2004年青少年年度風雲人物—美國中華國術聯盟
• 2003年青年全能國際冠軍—Sao Paulo-Brasil TWKF

When I was little, I thought that if I could get exceptionally good at Wushu, then I could become a Ninja Turtle or Power Ranger. Now that I'm older, I want to become a champion in Wushu—not just in the United States, but internationally.

I started training in traditional martial arts and Chinese Kenpo at the age of three. But when I turned eight, Jet Li and He Jing De changed my life. That's who I wanted to be. Today I want to be a hero for other kids like me. I hope to show people what Wushu is like, so that maybe I can help someone else start their journey, kind of like what Jet Li and He Jing De have done for me.

Wushu has done so much for me. It has given me discipline for school, driven me to work harder in school reports and tournament training, and has given me an advantage in other sports. Wushu has made me much more flexible and stronger than anyone my normal size and age.

Wushu is unlike anything I've ever experienced. It's unlike anything in the world. You have to have inner energy and passion to really portray it. Like in any sport, you can't just cruise through it. You have to push yourself to the extreme and think 'mind over matter.' If I could pursue anything else in the world, I wouldn't be able to pick, because nothing would benefit me the way Wushu has done for me.

我小時候認為，假使我夠把武術打得特別好，就可以轉化成卡通中的忍者龜或 Power Ranger；現在年紀比較大了，我希望成為武術運動頂尖選手，不只是在美國，而且能進軍國際。

我從三歲開始，就學習傳統的武術與中國 Kenpo，八歲時，李連杰與He Jing De 成為我的角色典範。現在我想成為其他孩童心目中的英雄，我希望去傳揚武術，所以可以幫助其他孩童，就如同李連杰與 He Jing De 幫助過我的一般。

武術對我影響甚大，它讓我在學校中懂得自律，讓我在課業上與競賽訓練中更加努力，並且在其他運動項目中表現更加優越。武術讓我在同年齡的朋友當中，更具柔韌性與壯碩。

武術和我過去經驗過的不太相同，全世界任何東西都不能跟它比。你必須要有內在能量與熱誠去真正體現它，如同其他運動項目，不能隨便敷衍了事。你必須超越極限，用內在精神力量去克服外在的困難。假如你讓我挑其他事去幹，我可能找不出來，因為沒有任何東西可以像武術一樣，對我益處這麼大。

23

Tiffany Reyes 蒂芬妮・蕊絲

Personal Reflections 個人感言

Date of Birth: December 26, 1979
Bachelor of Arts, UCLA
• 2005 U.S. Wushu Team Member
• 2005 Gold medals in Straight Sword, Spear & Other Empty Hand—
  Berkeley Chinese Martial Arts Tournament
• 2004 Gold medals in Straight Sword & Other Empty Hand—1st World
  Traditional Wushu Festival in Zhengzhou, China

生日：1979年12月26日
洛杉磯加州大學學士
• 2005年美國國家武術隊
• 2005年柏克萊武術競賽劍術、槍與自選式金牌得主
• 2004年中國鄭州第一屆世界傳統武術節大賽劍術與徒手項目金牌得主

"There are no shortcuts in Wushu,
as there are no shortcuts in life."

— *Tiffany Reyes*

「習武沒有捷徑，就像一般生活
中不能走捷徑。」

— 蒂芬妮・蕊絲

I started Wushu at age 21, what some may deem as late in life. However, it is important to understand that there are no shortcuts in Wushu, as there are no shortcuts in life. In order to achieve anything of value, you must put in the time and effort to achieve it. Once I decided that I wanted to become a serious, competitive Wushu athlete, I dedicated as much time as possible to training. When I wasn't physically training, I was thinking about my forms and movements and watching Wushu videos. I tried to spend as much time as possible absorbing knowledge and learning more.

An important lesson that I learned from Coach Li Jing that is not necessarily to train harder or more, but to train smart. That is, avoid any "mindless training." It's easy to fall in to a routine of going to practice and running through basics and movements. But it is important to make an extra effort to focus in on what it is you need to improve upon, and to concentrate all your efforts into a single thing at a time.

If I could offer advice to other aspiring Wushu athletes in regards to competition, I would like to explain that it's totally normal to feel nervous at competitions. However, the one thing that separates mature athletes from newer athletes is their ability to channel the nervousness away and perform their best. I found that the best way to overcome nervousness is to compete as much as possible, so that the feeling becomes more familiar to you. By competing often, you train both your body and your mind to handle the pressure.

我21歲才開始學習武術，對有些人來說能覺得太晚了。認清習武沒有捷徑是很重要的，就像一般生活中不能走捷徑；為達到有價值的人生，你必須付出時間與努力。一旦我認真思考想成為武術競技運動員，我即盡其所能在訓練上，當不在訓練時，我會思考自己的形式與動作，並且參看武術錄影帶，我會盡量利用時間吸收相關的知識。

我從李靜教練身上學到一個重要的功課，訓練不見得要死練，而是要聰明地去進行，也就是要避免「心不在焉的訓練」。當你訓練時，常會不經意地掉入無心的重覆學習，重要的是，應該集中精神與目標，在每一回的訓練中，在自己需要的單一項目上做改進。

假使我在競賽方面，能給其他武術運動員一些建議，那就是在競賽之前感覺緊張，是完全正常的，不過一名成熟的運動員與一名生手最大的差別，在於是否能把緊張轉化為能量，做最佳的表現。我發現克服緊張最佳的方法，就是盡量參加各種比賽，讓自己熟悉比賽的狀況，一旦經驗多了，你的身心狀態就會適應壓力。

David Chang 張世緯

"The people who succeed in life are those who have the tenacity to keep on going when the going gets rough."

— David Chang

「成功的人都是在事情變艱難的時候，而堅持繼續往前走。」

— 張世緯

Personal Reflections 個人感言

- 2001 Men's All-Around Champion—USAWKF National Championships
- Founder of Wushu Central, with appearances in *Qigong Kungfu Magazine*, *NBC News*, the *Discovery Channel*, and the *San Jose Mercury News*

- 2001年男子全能冠軍—美國武術功夫聯盟全國冠軍賽
- 創辦 Wushu Centeral 學校，是功夫氣功雜誌、國家廣播電視公司、Discovery 頻道、聖荷西信使報等媒體相繼報導的對象

I have always enjoyed teaching Wushu, ever since I started teaching the UC Berkeley Wushu Team. A few years ago, it dawned on me that I could actually teach and run a school as a career. I decided to go for it, beginning with just one student taught outdoors, to putting together a small school in my garage with about 20 students, to finally opening a full time school with currently over 175 students.

Opening and running a business is no small feat. It is said that when you own a business, you work 16 hours a day for yourself so that you don't have to work eight hours a day for somebody else. Going from 20 to 175 students in the span of just one and a half years was not an easy task, and it took a great deal of planning and labor to accomplish.

When I first started, I knew a lot about teaching great classes, working with both small children and older adults, and training athletes. On the other hand, I knew very little about successful business strategy. For the first year, I struggled along until I finally sought help from experts— people who had managed successful martial arts schools and other businesses.

One of those experts was my wife, Elizabeth. With her help, our business blossomed into a school with more students than ever before. Now, not only do we teach Wushu, but we also use it as a vehicle to help children learn important life skills and develop self-esteem. Adults benefit by losing weight, gaining flexibility and confidence, and getting into an exercise routine that they truly enjoy. To an aspiring Wushu athlete, I believe that the most critical element is to know what your dream is and why you want to pursue it. Then go for it and don't let anything stop you. The pursuit of anything difficult, such as national champion, will always be full of setbacks. Many times I see people who have inspirational goals, but as soon as they hit a wall, they give up and walk right away. If you want it enough, then you just can't quit. You have to break down that wall! This applies to everything in life.

There were many times when I was training hard or running the school and felt like giving up, but I persevered. After all, the people who succeed in life are those who have the tenacity to keep on going when the going gets rough.

我在柏克萊加州大學武術隊教課以來，就一直樂在其中。幾年前，我萌發一個念頭，其實，我為什麼不開一所武術學校，將它當成一種事業？所以我決定試試看。從在戶外教一名學生開始，轉移到在自己家中車庫教學的二十多名學生，最終開設全天候的武館，現在已收有175名學生。

開創與經營一個事業並不簡單，有人說，當你自己做老闆時，你要一天為自己工作16個小時，所以不必一天八小時去為別人幹活。在一年之內，從二十多名學生，增加到175名學生，不是件很容易的事。我做了大量的籌備工作，也耗去不少精力。

一開始，我對教課方法在行，學生中有孩童、也有成人，我也知道如何去訓練運動員；在另一方面，我對經營生意的策略，卻所知甚少。第一年，我自己孤軍奮鬥，最後找到了專家協助—這些專家曾經成功經營武館與其他生意。

專家當中，包括我的賢內助—伊麗莎白，因為有她的幫助，我們的武館業務蒸蒸日上，比過去收了很多學生。現在我們不單教課，同時也透過武術，來幫助孩童學習重要的生活技能與培養自尊。成人也受益無窮，包括減肥、增加身體柔韌度與自信心，也自運動中體會到真正的樂趣。

對任何有志向的武術運動員，我相信成功重要的因素，來自你有夢想，與瞭解自己一心追求的理由，然後全力以赴，不要讓任何事阻礙你前進。如果你的目標是全國冠軍，過程中當然會充滿挫折，很多時候，我見過很多人雖然有很好的目標，但當他們一碰壁，馬上放棄退縮。假如你真正想要達成夢想，你就不能輕言放棄，你必須將前面阻礙你的那座牆擊倒！這個原則可以運用到一般的生活。

有很多時候，我在接受嚴格訓練或經營武館時，放棄的念頭也會冒出來，但是我還是堅持下來了。畢竟，成功的人都是在事情變艱難的時候，而堅持繼續往前走。

第二部
Part II

Chinese Martial Arts
in the United States
武術在美國

Influx of Masters from Overseas
武術大師移民美國

In the early 1850s, Chinese adventurers embarked on bold, daring journeys across the Pacific Ocean. Lured by dreams of wealth, immigrants headed towards America with hopes of discovering gold. Thousands were enticed by the "Gold Mountain" in California, resulting in a large influx of Chinese immigrants to America. Martial arts culture was at first confined to the isolated Chinese population, but later blossomed in the 1900s.

By the 1990s, Chinese martial arts in the U.S. experienced tremendous growth. A number of talented masters arrived from overseas-including practitioners from Hong Kong, Taiwan, Mainland China and Southeast Asia. In this chapter, we introduce four outstanding masters who passed down the art of Wushu with different missions and channels in the United States.

Wah Lum Kung Fu School in Boston, MA
波士頓華林功夫武館

1850年代初期，中國人開始了大膽無畏的跨太平洋之旅，期望能在新大陸挖掘到黃金、找尋財富，數千人落腳在加州的「金山」，造成了中國人到美國的移民潮；武術也跟著被帶到美國，但是一開始，只是侷限在中國人的圈圈內，直到1900年代才真正向外發展。

1900年代，中國武術在美國經歷了很大的發展，一群天賦異秉的大師自海外湧進，中國、香港、台灣和東南亞等地區學習過武術的人，也大量來到美國。

Chinese Folktale: Praying Mantis Style
螳螂拳的由來

Approximately 400 years ago, there was a master named Wong Long who trained in the art of Shaolin Kungfu. Although he excelled in his art, one of his older Kungfu brothers was always slightly better. Time after time, Wong Long would test his skills against the other monks, only to be beaten by the same classmate.

Eventually, Wong Long decided that if he was ever going to beat his classmate, he would have to train even harder than his friend. One day while he was out in the forest training, he kneeled down to rest. Suddenly, a strange screaming noise rang from the trees. Upon closer inspection, he discovered the din coming from a cicada, which was being attacked by a praying mantis. Much to his surprise, the mantis was winning the fight over the much larger cicada.

Amazed that such a small insect could defeat a larger opponent, Wong Long captured the praying mantis and placed it in a cage. Day after day, he poked at it with a reed and carefully observed its reactions and movements.

Eventually Wong Long developed an array of basic movements that imitated the praying mantis. Determined, he practiced daily and incorporated these movements into his repertoire of techniques. He established a new style of Kungfu, which he called the Praying Mantis Style.

Soon after, he challenged his older classmate. However, he decided to keep his new discovery a secret. As the match began, Wong Long continuously used his eccentric fighting stance and unfamiliar fighting techniques. No matter what his classmate used against him, Wong Long always developed a new way of defending and countering. The classmate finally gave up, and Wong Long was declared the winner.

From that time on, all the Shaolin monks gathered together to help Wong Long develop his style even further. Today, there are twelve separate styles of Praying Mantis Kungfu.

螳螂拳是由王朗祖師創始於明末清初年間，距今約四百多年。雖然他在技藝上領先群倫，其中一個師兄永遠都比他厲害一點。日復一日，王朗總會與其他和尚比武試藝，但也總是敗給被同一個同門兄弟。

最後，王朗決定如果他真的要打敗這個師兄，必須要比同門有更艱辛的訓練。有一天，當他出外在森林中鍛鍊時，他一時跪下休息。突然間，他聽到一個尖銳的聲音穿過樹林。走進一點查看，他發現聲音是來自一隻被螳螂攻擊的蟬。令他非常驚訝的是，螳螂打敗了這個比牠身軀大很多的蟬。

訝異於這樣的小昆蟲竟然能擊倒較大的對手，王朗捉住螳螂，將牠關在籠子裡。每一天，他將一根稻桿伸進去，細心地觀察螳螂的反應和動作。

最後，王朗發展出一整套模仿螳螂的基本連續動作。決心致志，他每天練習，融合這些動作到他原有的功夫技巧當中。他自創了一個功夫的新招式，稱為螳螂拳法。

之後，他即刻向師兄挑戰，並保守自己這個新發明的秘密。比武開始，王朗持續地採用他不正規的打擊姿勢、不熟見的打擊技巧；不論他的師兄如何反抗他，王朗總能發展出一種新的防衛和反制方式。師兄最後放棄了打鬥，王朗獲得最後的勝利。

從此以後，所有的少林和尚聚在一起，幫助王朗將此武技更往前發展。如今，螳螂拳發展出十二種不同的拳式。

註：對於螳螂拳的起源，由於沒有確切資料可考，因而眾說紛紜，各種傳說很多，為螳螂拳增添一個神秘的色彩。

Grandmaster Pui Chan

陳培大師

Grandmaster Pui Chan is one of the early pioneers who spread the traditional Chinese martial arts to the non-Asian population. He is a sixth generation successor of the northern Praying Mantis Kung Fu System.

Pui Chan began his martial arts studies at the age of six as the last disciple of the Grandmaster Lee Kwan Shan. Although Pui Chan only attended school until he was nine years old, he taught himself to read and write in Chinese. He later fled to Hong Kong where he worked as a seaman; eventually he sailed to America with poor English and little money.

When the boat arrived in America, he jumped off in the middle of the night and swam ashore. He stayed in New York and worked in a restaurant, but later moved to Boston, where in 1970 he opened one of the first Kungfu schools in the area.

After a decade of hard work, he moved to Florida. In 1981 he built his own Wah Lum Temple of Orlando, one of the first schools of its kind to allow non-Chinese to learn this traditional art. Currently there are over 30 Wah Lum schools across the nation.

The popularity of the Wah Lum System Chinese Martial Arts in the U.S. is largely due to Grandmaster Chan's efforts over the last thirty years in promoting and teaching this traditional art. Many people are beginning to become aware of the wide variety of benefits from the training. Shifu Thomas Haase, who learned under Grandmaster Chan, says, "People see a very open and big-hearted person in Grandmaster Chan. Through his efforts, people are seeing someone from China who is open and willing to teach Americans on an even basis without prejudice. He has a big heart."

陳培大師是向非亞裔族群傳揚傳統中國武術的先鋒之一。他是第六代北螳螂功夫系統的傳承者。陳培六歲開始習武，是李昆山大師的最後弟子。雖然陳培直到九歲才上學，他以自學的方式，學會中文讀寫。後來他逃到香港，作海員為業；最後航行來到美國，身上只帶著很少的錢，並且講得一口很差的英語。

當船航抵美國，他在半夜跳船、游向岸邊。他待在紐約，在一家餐館工作，但後來搬到波士頓，1970年在當地開設了第一家功夫武館。在十年的辛苦經營後，他搬到佛羅里達州。1981年，他在佛羅里達州創建了華林寺，讓非中國人得以學習這項傳統的中國藝術。現在全美國已有三十多家的華林功夫武館。

華林系統在美國大受歡迎，要歸功於陳培師父在過去三十年間努力不懈地宣揚和傳授傳統功夫。越來越多的人開始知道，功夫訓練可以帶來的很多不同的益處。跟隨著陳大師學習的唐夏士師父說：「人們在陳大師身上看到了一個心胸開放、寬大胸懷的人。經由他的努力，看到一個來自中國的人，如此開放，願意在公平的基礎上，無偏見地教授美國人。他真是有一顆寬大的心。」

Sifu Mimi Chan

陳美美師父

"I will stay at the Wah Lum Temple and teach to ensure that the next generation will be able to carry on the traditions of my father."

—*Mimi Chan*

「我的長期目標是留在華林寺教授學生，以確保下一代能傳承我父親寶貴的功夫傳統。」

—陳美美

Mimi Chan began her training under her father, Pui Chan, at the age of three. She has competed since she was twelve years old, and has received numerous accolades from the professional martial arts community.

Her highly revered performances have been marketed in a variety of television and film shows, business conventions, and public events. She was chosen as the model and martial arts video reference for Disney's *Mulan*. She has also appeared in movies and television shows such as *Mortal Kombat Conquest* and *Sheena*.

Although Mimi never truly sought a career in movies, she says she would love to do more film work if offered the chance. Her long-term goals are to stay at the Wah Lum Temple and teach to ensure that the next generation will be able to carry on the traditions of her father.

陳美美三歲時，在父親陳培的訓練下開始習武，十二歲時，就開始參加比賽，而且得到了專業武術團體的推崇。

她的表演在許多不同的電視、電影、商業會議和公共場合中出現。在迪士尼的卡通《花木蘭》一片中，主角花木蘭的造型與武術動作，乃是根據陳美美的外貌與武術動作，透過錄影與電腦技術合成，製作成動畫片的。她曾在不同的電影和電視秀中，例如《Mortal Kombat Conquest》和《Sheena》一劇。

雖然陳美美從沒有去主動去追尋電影事業，她說若有機會的話，也不會加以排斥。她的長期目標是留在華林寺教授學生，以確保下一代能傳承她父親寶貴的功夫傳統。

Master Hao Zhi Hua (Patti Li)

郝致華教練

Master Hao Zhi Hua started her Wushu training at the age of nine as a member of the first generation of the Beijing Wushu Team at the Beijing Sports Academy under the instruction of director Wu Bin, a pioneer of modern Wushu in China.

By 1983, Hao Zhi Hua won the title of China's All-Around Women's Champion three years in a row. At the Chinese Olympics also known as the National Athletic Tournament held in Shanghai, Hao Zhi Hua won six gold medals out of the ten events that were taken by the Beijing women's team. She had won an unmatched total of six events including long fist, single broadsword, double broadsword, staff, sparring set, and eagle claw.

She was honored as one of the Top Ten Athletes in China along with Jet Li (still the only Wushu practitioners to receive this award) and a Wu Ying Wushu Master Award (The Highest Ranked Belt in Wushu).

Featured in numerous publications, she has toured the world as a living symbol of Chinese martial arts excellence. As master teacher at Wushu West in Berkeley, she has trained Wushu champions, athletes, entertainers and martial arts teachers. She is dedicated to promoting and manifesting the highest standards of Wushu students with championship dreams.

"The discipline and confidence developed while practicing wushu is applicable to everyday life."
— *Master Patti Li*

「從習武中發展出的自律與自信，可以運用到每一天的生活當中。」
— 郝致華教練

郝致華教練九歲開始，被選入北京體育運動學校，師從現代武術開創者吳彬，是北京武術隊的第一批專業運動員。

郝致華在1983年之前，曾連續三年獲得全中國女子全能武術冠軍。在上海舉辦、有「中國奧運」之稱的全國運動大會中，北京武術女隊於十項競賽裡獲得十面金牌，其中六面金牌由郝致華奪得，包括：長拳、單刀、雙刀、棍、對練（單刀對雙槍）與前所未有的鷹爪拳。她與李連杰同時被列為「中國十大最佳運動員」（目前唯一得到此榮譽的武術運動員），她同時獲得武英級武術教練獎（最高的武術稱號）。

郝致華在不同的刊物中被介紹，曾到世界各地做表演，是優秀中國武術的代表。做為加州柏克萊 Wushu West 武術學校的總教練，郝致華訓練出無數的武術冠軍、運動員、演藝人員與教練。她全心全意以最高的標準，栽培有冠軍夢的武術學生。

Coach Li Jing

李靜教練

"I started wushu from age six. I don't consider myself the best, but I am the one who always works the hardest."

— *Coach Li Jing*

「我從六歲開始習武，我不認為自己是最優秀的，但永遠卻是最認真的。」

— 李靜教練

Li Jing is another example of a highly qualified athlete who immigrated to the U.S. By coaching the UC Berkeley Wushu Team, she transformed local students into top Wushu athletes.

Li Jing has over 20 years of martial arts experience and ranked as one of the Top Six Female Kungfu/Wushu Athletes in China. As a professional athlete of the Beijing Wushu Team, she trained under Jet Li's former coach Wu Bin. She has premiered in a number of films and commercials, and was the Lead Stunt Double for the Women's World Cup 2003 commercial. She has also been featured in the *PBS* documentary *Made in Hong Kong* and the Sony music video *Double Blade* starring Jay Chou. In addition, she coached Wushu teams in Taiwan, Singapore, Australia, and Poland.

李靜是另一位移民到美國的傑出武術運動員，她擔任過柏克萊加州大學武術隊教練，將學生訓練成頂尖的武術選手。

李靜的武術經驗超過二十年，在中國名列為六大女子武術/功夫選手之一。身為北京武術隊的專業選手，她也受到名師吳彬教練的青睞與嚴格的訓練。她曾出現在許多是電影和廣告中，做過2003年女子足球世界杯廣告的替身。李靜是美國公共電視台《香港製》紀錄片中的主角之一，並在周杰倫為主角的新力音樂錄影帶「雙刃」中演出。另外，她還擔任過台灣、新加坡、澳洲和波蘭的國家武術隊教練。

National China Wushu Team Performs at the White House
中國國家武術隊在白宮演出

In 1972, President Richard M. Nixon formally invited the China Wushu Team to tour America. In order to identify the finest young Wushu athletes in the country, the Chinese government implemented a talent search. In 1974, the athlete-delegates visited the White House and various cities around the world. Among these athletes was current Hollywood star Jet Li, who was just nine years old at the time.

Another testament to China's commitment to opening up its doors to the outside world was Grandmaster Daoyun Chen, a seventh degree black belt. Coach Chen was the women's captain of this legendary team. During this historical exchange, Wushu gained widespread coverage and praise from major media outlets such as the *New York Times* and *Washington Post*.

1972年，美國總統尼克森正式邀請中國國家武術隊到美國演出；中國政府為了篩選全國最優秀的年輕武術選手，曾進行了一場全國性大規模的人才選拔。1974年，這些萬中挑一的優秀運動員，代表中國訪問了白宮和世界大城市。選手當中，有一位就是現在的好萊塢動作片巨星李連杰，當時的他，只有九歲。

中國當年下定決心對外開放，精挑萬選出來的中國國家武術隊，由現時的黑帶七段陳道雲教練擔任隊長。在這個歷史性的文化之旅中，美國主流媒體《紐約時報》和《華盛頓郵報》等都做了廣泛的報導和予以讚揚。

Jet Li (first row on the left), Dao Yun Chen (second on the right) and China Wushu Team members performed at the White House. 陳道雲（右二）李連杰（前排左一）等一起到白宮演出。

Wushu Meets Hollywood
武術進軍好萊塢

Wushu remained fairly unknown in the U.S. until the 1970s. In February 1972, the original ninety-minute pilot film *Kung Fu* hit American TV screens. The weekly series, starring David Carradine, grew to become the number-one rated show in the United States. Martial artist Bruce Lee also later landed roles in Hollywood; among these was his signature film *Enter the Dragon* (1973). With the legacy of Bruce Lee, martial arts popularity exploded in the 1970s, sparking a craze in the United States.

Since then, Wushu has steadily gained popularity in Hollywood with the help of film personalities like Jet Li and Jackie Chan. Moreover, Ang Lee's *Crouching Tiger Hidden Dragon* made its successful debut in 2000, capturing four Academy awards and two Golden Globe awards. Zhang Yimou's successful film *Hero* topped the box-office for two straight weekends after its belated debut in August 2004. Other Hollywood movies, such as *The Matrix* and *Once Upon a Time in China*, have also incorporated Wushu into their action scenes.

1970年代，武術在美國仍是默默無聞。1972年2月，九十分鐘劇情片《功夫》在美國電視上播映。這個每週一次的影片，由大衛卡洛丁主演，後來位居美國分級片的第一名。之後，李小龍在好萊塢聲名大噪，其中一個代表作是1973年的《龍爭虎鬥》，因著李小龍傳奇，中國武術在1970年代，在美國造成一股勢不可擋的風潮。

從此之後，武術靠著李連杰、成龍等電影巨星的掘起，持續不斷得到好萊塢的青睞。尤有甚者，李安導演的《臥虎藏龍》在2000年成功地得到四項奧斯卡金像獎和兩項金球獎。導演張藝謀膾炙人口的電影《英雄》在2004年8月首映後，連續兩週盤踞美國電影票房的第一名。其他好萊塢電影，如《駭客任務》和《黃飛鴻》，都在打鬥場面中明顯應用了武術的技巧與招式。

Bruce Lee's portrait 李小龍畫像
Painted by Jessica Liu 劉玉寧作

龙

Eric Johnsbone
艾瑞克·鍾斯本

Arthur Chen
陳禮華

Collegiate Wushu
大學武術社團

In 1922, the Chinese Physical Cultural Association founded the first club to practice Kungfu in organized classes. Established in Honolulu, it promoted physical fitness but excluded non-Asians. In 1957, TInn Chan Lee, a Taiji specialist, became the first Chinese instructor to open his teachings to the general public.

In the early 1980s, Wushu remained relatively unknown among college students. Various collegiate Wushu clubs existed throughout the country, but clubs struggled with hiring qualified coaches, maintaining classes, and organizing competitions. Some of the more popular clubs of the time included the University of California-Berkeley Club (Cal Wushu), University of Oregon Club, UCLA, and UC Irvine.

Since then, collegiate Wushu has spread to other campuses, including Stanford University, Harvard University, Ohio State University, University of Maryland, University of Virginia, etc. In California, annual collegiate competitions promote Chinese martial arts and team unity. UC Berkeley also holds an annual Chinese Martial Arts Tournament in April, which is entirely run with the help of volunteers.

1922年，中國體育文化協會成立了第一個有組織的功夫社團。它創始於檀香山，推廣體能健身，不拒絕非亞裔族群的參與。1957年，太極專家李庭晨是第一位將他的課程開放給所有社會大眾的華裔教師。

1980年代初期，武術在大學生當中，仍相當無聞。雖然武術社團林立在不同的校園內，但很難聘請合格的教練、維持課程與組織競賽。當時還是有幾個比較熱門的社團，像柏克萊加州大學、奧瑞岡大學、洛杉磯加州大學和爾灣加州大學等的武術社團。

後來，大學武術漸推廣到其他校園，包括史丹福大學、哈佛大學、俄亥俄州立大學、馬里蘭州立大學、維吉尼亞州立大學等。在加州，每年舉辦的各種大學比賽，發揚了中國武術和團隊合作精神，規模較大的柏克萊加州大學武術大賽在每年4月舉辦，全藉由義工的幫助籌備與完成。

Coach Phillip Wong and Zhang Hong Mei

菲利普・黃教練與張宏梅教練

S tanford Wushu is a fairly new student club that began practicing in 1997. Currently, Stanford Wushu has a 100+ membership that grows with each year. Master Phillip Wong and his wife Zhang Hong Mei are the head coaches of Stanford Wushu Club.

史 丹福武術社團成立於1997年，現在已有一百多位成員。菲利普・黃與張宏梅夫婦是史丹福武術社團的總教練。

Coach Phillip Wong

Phillip Wong has participated in thirteen National and International Grand Championships as a champion Member of the U.S. National Wushu Team. At the 2nd International Wushu Games in 1986, He won a silver medal for his all-around performance. He has been featured on many magazine covers in the U.S., China, Italy and Japan, and was nominated as Competitor of the Year in 1987 by *Inside KungFu* Magazine. He has performed in motion capture studios for numerous video games, such as *Tekken 2 & 3 and Mace: The Dark Age*. In addition, he has starred in various Asian films and choreographed many feature films in the USA.

Coach Zhang Hong Mei

Born in Beijing, China, Zhang Hong Mei began Wushu at nine, after being chosen from thousands of children to train in an elite sports program at Shi Cha Hai. She developed into one of China's top athletes, winning gold medals in Bagua, sparring routines, and double straight swords at national competitions. As a member of China's national team, Zhang Hong Mei captured gold in women's straight sword in the 1st International Games held in Xian, China. By invitation, Zhang taught Wushu and Taiji in Japan. She has appeared in dozens of international magazine covers and has been featured in numerous films, videos and TV shows.

菲利普・黃教練

菲利普・黃是美國國家武術隊成員，曾參加過全美與國際間的十三次比賽，他是1986年第二屆國際武術競賽的十項全能銀牌得主。菲利普・黃曾是美國、中國、義大利、日本等國的雜誌封面人物，也被美國《Inside KungFu》雜誌選為1987年年度運動員。他曾為不同的電玩做武術動作示範、在不同的亞洲電影演出，同時也在許多美國的電影動作片中擔任武術指導。

張宏梅教練

張宏梅生於北京，九歲起即開始學習武術，從數千名應試者中脫穎而出，在石剎海武術學校接受訓練。她是中國最傑出的武術運動員之一，曾在全國性的比賽中取得八卦掌、對練與雙劍冠軍。做為北京武術代表隊成員，她曾在西安舉辦的第一屆世界武術比賽獲雙劍冠軍。

她代表中國至世界各地三十多個國家做巡迴演出，也被日本請去教導武術與太極。張宏梅是數十本各國雜誌的封面人物，也在眾多的電影、錄影片與電視節目中露面。

Thomas Chi 遲佑吉

"Training is more about facing the mental challenge of discipline, understanding the meaning behind martial arts, and learning about oneself in the process of training."

— *Thomas Chi*

「武術訓練是一種自律與心理挑戰，學習到其背後的深厚含意後，可以藉由過程來瞭解自己。」

— 遲佑吉

Personal Reflections 個人感言

Date of Birth: April 18, 1978
BA and MA degrees, Stanford University
UCSF School of Medicine
• 2003 1st Place Beginner's Adult Long Fist, Broadsword, and Staff—
  Chinese American Athletic Tournament

生日：1978年4月18日
史丹福大學學士與碩士
舊金山州立大學醫學院學生
• 2003年北加州華人運動會成人初級組長拳、刀、棍三項金牌得主

When I first started Wushu, I was surrounded by people who had trained for years. Their athleticism, flexibility, and grace were truly inspiring. It was a level of physical prowess that I hoped to strive for.

Training was extremely difficult, especially near the beginning. I learned to move in ways that I'd never done before, and I worked my body harder than ever. At the beginning, most of my thoughts and feelings regarding Wushu were about the physical aspects. I was sore everyday, and I only focused on physical goals that I hoped to achieve, such as higher levels of flexibility and strength.

Since that time, however, I've started to regard Wushu in a different manner. Training is more about facing the mental challenge of discipline, understanding the meaning behind martial arts, and learning about one's self in the process of training. There are dimensions of martial arts that permeate throughout life, going beyond the physical body, and those are the things I think about more often nowadays.

I would encourage other children to learn wushu. A lot of that is because I think it can teach them about respect, about discipline, about not being afraid of challenges, about confidence, and also keep them physically fit. It's truly a marvelous art, and I would be the first to recommend it to other people.

在我剛學武術的時候，班上同學多已訓練多年，他們的運動精神、柔韌度與優雅，時時激勵著我，這些態度與本事，是我渴望達成的目標。

訓練過程是很困難的，特別是在一開始，我學著如何去轉動自己的身體，很多運用身體的方式是我從未嘗試過的，我比過去使上更多的勁。一開始，我對武術的想法和感受是，它僅是一種體能訓練，我每天練得全身酸痛，全神貫注去加強自己的柔韌性與力量。

可是之後，我對武術產生了不同的體會。武術訓練其實是一種自律與心理挑戰，學習到其背後的深厚含意後，可以藉由過程來瞭解自己。武術在很多方面可運用到日常生活，它是超越體能的，這些是我現在體會較多的。

我會鼓勵其他孩子學習武術，因為武術可以讓他們學習到尊敬他人、自律、不怕挑戰、自信與保持身體健康。武術是一門很了不起的藝術，我會是將它介紹給其他人的第一人。

Alfred Hsing and Alvin Hsing
邢思杰、邢思作兄弟

Alfred Hsing 邢思杰

Personal Reflections 個人感言

Date of Birth: November 23, 1983
Economics Major, UCLA
• 1999 and 2000 Grand Champion at Martial Arts World Cup
• Ranked third at Nationals in Contemporary Open Weapons

生日：1983年11月23日
洛杉磯加州大學經濟系學生
• 1990年與2000年世界武裝盃總冠軍
• 《現代武術自選器械》全美排名第三

"When I find myself not focusing, I remember the principles of Wushu, which always help me to stay on the right track."

— *Alfred Hsing*

「當我發現自己注意力無法集中時，我會聯想到習武的種種原則，指導我走向正確的方向。」

— 邢思杰

What I like about Wushu is the feeling it gives me. Not only is it aesthetically pleasing, but it also strengthens me physically and works out the entire body. I like the feeling of being really sore after a good workout.

Practicing Wushu has allowed me to meet a lot of dedicated people, which inspires me to work harder in all aspects of life. When I find myself not focusing, I remember the principles of Wushu, which always help me to stay on the right track.

For me, Wushu in college is the biggest challenge. In college, there are so many distractions that pull me away from Wushu, such as academics, jobs, and social events. College is a transitory phase from education to the workforce, and there's a lot that needs to be prepared for.

When I was in high school, I lived a simple routine. I went to school, ate food, and practiced Wushu. Today there are the pressures of college, but in any case, I believe it is a test of dedication and motivation for me."

我熱愛武術，因為它帶給我美好的感受。它不只外觀優美，而且能強化體能，是一種全身的鍛鍊。我喜歡那種鍛鍊過後全身酸痛的感覺。

習武讓我認識許多優秀的人，激勵我在生活各方面更加努力。當我發現自己注意力無法集中時，我會聯想到習武的種種原則，指導我走向正確的方向。

對我而言，一邊讀大學、一邊繼續習武，是很大的挑戰。在大學中，好多雜事讓我無法專心習武，例如學校的課業、工作與社交生活等；大學是從學校走向社會的過度階段，有好多事需要做準備。

當我在讀高中時，生活較單純，上學、吃飯、練武，現在唸大學，壓力就比較大，但無論如何，我相信這是我對武術專注學習與持續努力的一項考驗。

Michele Chen 陳盈盈

"Learning Wushu has given me a sense of pride in my own culture, allowing me to reminisce the past and appreciate my ethnicity."

— *Michele Chen*

「習武讓我以自身的文化為榮，緬懷過去，並重視自己華裔的背景。」

— 陳盈盈

Personal Reflections 個人感言

Date of Birth: January 8, 1988
Lynbrook High School, California
• 2005 Miss Teen Asian America
• 2004 Miss Teen Chinatown, San Francisco
• 2004 1st Place Advanced Straightsword, Spear—Inaugural Tai-chi for Fitness Championships

生日：1988年1月8日
加州林布魯克高中生
• 2005年亞裔妙齡小姐
• 2004年舊金山華埠妙齡小姐
• 2004年聖荷西州立大學首屆太極武術冠軍賽高級組劍術/槍術冠軍

When I was young, my mother exposed me to many possible extracurricular activities. Out of these hobbies, I managed to try and quit the saxophone, piano, ballet, Chinese dance, tennis, abacus, and drums. None of these activities kept me interested enough. They became routine, and one by one I quit them all.

One day, I came across an intriguing martial arts film. My eyes grew wide as I pictured myself leaping from roof to roof, and gliding across lakes, just like the actor. From that day on, I decided that I wanted to be a super wushu woman, so I began Wushu training.

But after training for the first time, I grew disappointed. 'Why aren't they flying?' I questioned aloud, referring to the advanced students. My instructor chuckled and replied, 'Wushu isn't about flying and walking on water. It's about building character and willpower, and achieving what you want through discipline.' I was disappointed that I would never learn to fly, but I continued learning.

In the long run, Wushu has not only taught me about discipline and respect, it has also taught me a lot about my Chinese ethnicity. Growing up Asian in America doesn't allow enough time to truly explore what our culture have to offer. Learning Wushu has given me a sense of pride in my own culture, allowing me to reminisce the past and appreciate my ethnicity.

當我小的時候，媽媽讓我接觸很多課外活動，在眾多活動中，我陸續嘗試了薩克斯風、鋼琴、芭蕾、中國民族舞蹈、網球、算盤與擊鼓。可是沒有一樣讓我真正對其發生興趣，久而久之，它們都變得很單調，一一逐漸被我放棄了。

偶爾一天，我看到一部很有趣的武俠片，我睜大著眼睛，想像自己就如片中的演員飛簷走壁，之後，我想做個超級女子，所以開始我的習武生涯。

第一次到武館，我卻感到萬分失望，指著那些高級班的學生，拉開嗓門問老師：「他們為什麼不能飛？」老師笑著回答：「武術不是用來高空騰飛或水上穿行的，它是用來發展個人特質與意志力，透過自律，達到個人的理想。」雖然我對自己無法學到在高空穿梭來去感到失望，但是還是繼續學習武術。

長期以來，武術讓我學到自律與尊敬他人，同時讓我對自己的中國文化有更多的瞭解，在美國長大的亞裔，實在沒有足夠的機會瞭解自己。習武，讓我以自身的文化為榮，緬懷過去，並重視自己華裔的背景。

第三部
Part III

Wushu Training
武術訓練

Pushing the Limits of Human Potential
挑戰人體的極限

Hong Dao Wushu Academy
弘道武術學院

Under the bright afternoon sun, groups of youth are enduring rigorous Wushu training at the spacious Jollyman Park in Cupertino, California. They are students of Coach Dao Yun Chen. Some are members of the United States Wushu Team; others are gold medal champions, yet others come from a variety of top-ranking universities and local colleges, such as MIT, UC San Francisco, UC Berkeley, UCLA, and De Anza College.

The warm-up for outdoor Wushu training is an involved process. It includes running for 3 or 4 laps around the park, followed by frog leaps, and then numerous rounds of basics training. After roughly 20 minutes, the students are soaked in sweat and breathing heavily. Strangely, no one is complaining; everyone is focused and ready.

In China, Coach Dao Yun Chen is known as the "Gold Medal Factory." For her, Wushu is the trademark of traditional Chinese culture. It is a part of the very fabric of Chinese society and landscape. Although Wushu has evolved into a modern sport, it is Coach Chen's hope that it will become a world-renowned sport as well. "America is the world leader in sports. I fervently hope that with its strength, it will help spread Wushu to the rest of the world," she says.

Coach Dao Yun Chen has been involved in professional Wushu training and coaching for over 40 years. She won the National All-Around Wushu Championship for 13 consecutive years in China, and served as the team captain of the renowned Chinese National Wushu Team in 1974. As for training students in the United States, Coach Chen says, "Initially, I felt that American kids were a bit more arrogant, but I found that they were in fact hardworking and diligent. I truly admire them."

Through her coaching, she has become much more than just an instructor. With the help of supportive parents and the community at large, she and the students have helped each other grow and learn over the course of time. Although Wushu is extremely demanding, it is also the ultimate expression of the harmonious blend of power and beauty. Wushu has become the focal point of so many lives, because it challenges the body to the limit to achieve its true potential.

豔陽天下,一群精力充沛的青少年在北加州庫比蒂諾市諾大的Jollyman公園內,接受最嚴格的武術訓練。他們是傑出武術教練陳道雲的學生,其中有最近在東岸嚴格選拔出來的美國國家武術隊運動員,多位在各項國際與地方武術比賽的金牌選手,也有來自耶魯大學、舊金山大學醫學院、柏克萊大學、洛杉磯加大等校的高材生。

戶外武術訓練暖身運動之一,是先繞大操場跑三、四圈,來回蛙跳,做十幾趟來回基本功。20分鐘下來,雖然汗流浹背、氣喘如牛,可是無人叫累、喊苦,個個甘之如飴。武術的魅力可見一斑。

中國武術八段的陳道雲教練,在中國有「金牌加工廠」的稱號。她說,武術是中國傳統文化的招牌,它在中國的土地生根,像土壤、空氣與水,已深入人心。武術已發展成現代的體育項目,但是要走向世界,還需規範化、系統化。「美國是世界的巨富、體育龍頭,我希望在美國能凝聚力量,把中國武術幾代人的心血與奮鬥傳揚世界。」

陳道雲在武術教學方面已有四十多年經驗,她在中國連續十三年贏得全國武術冠軍,1974年中國國家武術隊到美國表演時,她擔任隊長。對於訓練美國的孩子,陳道雲說:「我當初以為美國孩子比較有驕氣,但發現他們都是搏命學習、毫不偷懶,我覺得很欣慰。」

難得的是,她與學生的精神相互感染、彼此反饋、激發潛能,師生都有著不甘示弱的進取心,形成一股奮發向上的氣息;而學生家長也是全力支持配合,渾然是一個融洽的武術大家庭。很明顯的,武術難度極高,卻能表現動感,是力與美的結合;而武術挑戰人體能量的極限,則是師生對其樂此不疲的原因。

Recipe for Success
成功的要素

U.S. Wushu Team Coach Dao Yun Chen says that there are three stages to reaching the ultimate level in Wushu training. First, practice and persistence are essential. A student must be willing to train hard with the aid of scientific practices, and must be passionate enough to incorporate Wushu into their daily lives. The next ingredient to success, she believes, is the importance of a strong foundation. An athlete's basic foundation is like that of a well built house, able to withstand the test of time. "Jet Li's incredible Wushu skills come from his more than ten years of diligent practice," she says. Lastly, students must possess a natural understanding of their abilities. Refining natural abilities along with diligent training and a willingness to learn will lead to ultimate success.

陳道雲教練指出,要達到武術功底的最高境界有三步曲:一、刻苦耐勞:要能苦練、巧練、科學化地練。肯付出、投入,拳不離手。練功時間無所不在,融入生活動靜之中。勤奮不偷懶,隨時動。二、扎實的基本功:非花拳繡腿,武術運動員的功底有如房子的地基越牢,使用越久。基本功好,萬年不退色,想成功沒有捷徑。「李連杰能成功,武打逼真,叫人看了舒服,這是他幾十年鍛鍊與塑造出來的儀表,其氣質、神韻、精力,均與眾不同。手眼身法均是內在的的表現。」三、悟性:有先天與後天的區別,每人打出娘胎就不同,有些人對武術感覺特別好,靈感、眼神、講話神態是先天遺傳下來的。有些人後天擅長學習模仿、表現,將眾家之長據為己有。站在塔尖上的尖子,必能吃苦。先天加後天,虛心學習,就能成功。

Opposite: **Grandmaster Dao Yun Chen**
陳道雲教練

Lee Hsieh
謝禮

"The journey of a thousand miles begins with a first step."

— *Lao Tse*

「千里之行，始於足下。」

— 老子

What Age is Best for Learning Wushu?
最適合習武的年齡？

Although there is no "perfect age" to begin training, several coaches recom mend students to begin training from a young age, anywhere from six t thirteen. Mimi Chan, who was a martial arts video reference for Disney's anima tion *Mulan*, says, "Obviously, being younger is a good age to start, but it is neve too late. People of all ages, ethnicities, weights, and genders should try Kungfu Everyone does it for different reasons and gains different benefits. You can be a good as your body and mind will allow you to be."

其實沒有所謂的「最適合習武的年齡」，但是許多師父與教練都認為，愈早愈好，最好是在六歲至十三歲之間。在迪士尼「花木蘭」動畫片中擔任主角造型與武打本尊的陳美美說：「當然，愈早愈有利，但卻永不嫌遲。任何年齡、族裔背景、體重、性別的人，都應該嘗試武術。不同原因的學習，都可以獲得不同的益處。只要身心狀況許可，都能達到目標。」

Basic Wushu Movements and Curriculum
武術的基本動作與訓練項目

Five Basic Stances 五個基本步形
Demonstrates by Coach Zhang Hong Mei
張宏梅教練示範

Horse stance 馬步

Front/Bow stance 弓步

Drop stance 仆步

Empty stance 虛步

Sit/Crouch stance 歇步

Fist 拳

Palm 掌

Hook 勾

Demonstrates by Jeffrey Lee
李明道示範

Basic Kicks 基本腿法

Leg Raise/Front Stretch Kick 正踢腿

Heel Kick 蹬腿

Toe Kick 彈腿

Side Leg Kick 側踢腿

Side Kick 踹腳

Inside Crescent 裏合腿

Outside Crescent 外擺腿

Front Slapping Leg Raise 單拍腳

Jumps 跳躍動作

Jumping Inside Kick 旋風腿

Jumping Outside Kick 外百連

Jumping Front Kick 二起腳

Butterfly 旋子

Aerial 側空翻

Butterfly Twist 三百六十度空翻

720 七百二十度空翻

Sweeps 掃腿

Front Sweep 前掃腿

Back Sweep 後掃腿

Weapons and Handforms 器械與手型

Long Fist 長拳

Southern Fist 南拳

Broadsword 刀

Straightsword 劍

Staff/Cudgel 棍

Spear 槍

Other major disciplines 其他

Tumbling Boxing 地躺拳

Eagle Claw 鷹爪拳

Monkey Fist and Monkey Cudgel 猴拳與猴棍

Praying Mantis 螳螂拳

Drunken Style 醉拳

9-section Whip 九節鞭

Double Sword and Double Broadsword 雙劍與雙刀

Long Tassel Straightsword 長穗劍

Long-handled Scimitar 關刀

Rope and Dart 繩與飛鏢

Hook Sword 勾劍

3-section Cudgel 三節棍

Contemporary Wushu Styles
現代武術形式

Wushu encompasses hundreds of styles, but the "core curriculum" of contemporary Wushu training can be categorized into the different styles depicted below. Beginners typically receive introductory lessons in the major styles and then later specialize in certain categories to match their abilities, personalities, and tastes. Most students concentrate on one style of each hand form, short weapon, and long weapon. The combination is often chosen at the instructor's discretion.

武 術包含上百種的形式，而現代武術訓練的主要課程可以分成以下數種。初學者通常從基本功學起，之後再根據自己的能力、個人特性與喜好做進一步的選擇。大部分的學生以其中三項專心操練，包括手型、短兵器與長兵器，並且多半由教練代為選擇。

Jack Tu
涂聖成

	Northern System 北派	Southern System 南派
Hand Forms 手型	Long Fist 長拳	Southern Fist 南拳
Short Weapon 短兵器	Broadsword 刀	Southern Broadsword 南刀
	Straightsword 劍	
Long Weapon 長兵器	Spear 槍	Southern Staff 南棍

Opposite: **Sifu Fei Chen and Melody Chung**
陳飛師父與鍾珮璇

Jeffrey Lee 李明道

"Through Wushu I have become a more compassionate, more focused, and more confident person."

— *Jeffrey Lee*

「從武術訓練當中，我變得更加富有同情心、注意力更加集中與更具自信心。」

— 李明道

Personal Reflections 個人感言

Date of Birth: September 10, 1988
Saratoga High School, California
• 2004 1st Place Intermediate Straightsword, Ages 13-17—UC Berkeley Chinese Martial Arts Tournament

生日：1988年9月10日
北加州沙拉度加高中學生
• 2004年柏克萊中國武術大賽—13歲至15歲中級組劍術冠軍

Crilik! A crushing blow, snapping his opponent's knee in the wrong direction. Another man races towards Jet Li and aggresses with a flying jump kick. Whipow! Jet Li delivers another direct hit to this aerial foe with one sweeping arched kick from the ground; he remains unfazed. Jet Li continues on to demolishing his enemies one, two, three, or even four at a time. WhapWhapWhap!!! Three kicks to three more foes, sending them flying in different directions, accompanied by shouts of pain!

As a 4 year old, I used to stand in front of the television mimicking every motion of the Chinese superman. To me, anyone who could defeat their enemies utilizing the superior art of Kung Fu was a hero. I thought that beating people up and looking stylish while you did it was all there was to Kung Fu, and all that it was good for. Even though not too much time has passed since those days, my views of Kung Fu have drastically changed and I have found what Wushu means to me.

Watching Kung Fu films and listening to stories sparked my initial interest in Wushu. Coupled with my love for Chinese culture and customs, my desire to learn was unparalleled by anything else I've ever wanted to do in my life. Soon, Kung Fu became my passion and appreciated the discipline martial arts training required. However, with the joy of Wushu, came the inevitable struggles and hardships.

I had just finished my third year of Wushu when I received the opportunity to train at the Shi Cha Hai Athletic School in Beijing. Understanding that this would be the chance of a lifetime, I trained with all my heart in the weeks prior to the trip. I wanted to sow all the right seeds in America, that way I could harvest the sweet fruit of progress in China. This trip meant that I would have the chance to improve, to win the glory of gold medals and ultimately have a shot at the United States team trials.

Little did I know that in my feelings of joy and hope, I would reap the whirlwind. I failed to remember than the higher I jumped, the farther I would fall; I realized too late and I proceeded to fall on a pointed toe and snap my ankle beyond the safe range of motion, to say the least, to a not-so-satisfying wet popping sound. I was so stunned by my folly that I did not even feel pain. All I knew in my mind was failure, defeat, and hopelessness. I knew in my broken heart that all my dreams were crushed.

I debated whether I should continue with my original plan. At first I was skeptical of what I could gain from this trip; it would be a shame to waste both time and money if I was unable to practice, but my friends and family supported me and encouraged me to go, so I decided to experience the hot and sweltering over that of air-conditioned summer school classroom. During the four weeks at the sport's school, I trained hard and made friends that would last a lifetime. Although I could not train to the extent that I would have liked, I pushed myself as hard as I could, learning every detail and nuance more than I actually trained so I could practice these new skill sets after my ankle healed.

In some ways, my disabling injury had its silver lining, for my physical restriction allowed me to sit back and see athleticism from a wider perspective. Sitting on the sideline forced me to focus more on observing the training of my peers and role models. I learned to always focus on the target even if it is imaginary, to never lose sight of the application of the movement. I also learned that dynamism key.

During my third week, as I was practicing a technique in front of the mirror in the Wushu hall, frustrated with my debilitating injuries and angry at myself, I sheathed my sword and sat despairingly down on a bench. I suddenly heard a loud music of Chinese drums, flutes, and string instruments. Scanning the room for the source of such vibrant sound, my eyes soon came upon the most impressive display of speed, flexibility, concentration, and balance in a choreographed and synchronized tai chi form. The performer's every motion was so fluid and executed with such precision and perfection that I could only gape in awe, completely spellbound by the dynamic contrast of strength and flexibility melding seamlessly together.

Finally, when the music subsided and the performer left the mat, I noticed that on the back wall behind which the girl had exhibited her last tai chi stance hung the Chinese flag, juxtaposed in between two Chinese words "Martial Spirit".

In that instant, I had an epiphany. I realized what a martial artist personifies and what Wushu means. Martial arts isn't about looking cool, flexing muscles, or having the ability to beat opponents. Rather, the true spirit of Martial arts lies in taking responsibility of the power through exercising restraint. Above all, martial art teaches honor, justice, discipline, and self-control by underscoring the importance of balance, form, concentration, focus, and tenacity.

The hero is not born of the Kung Fu he knows, but of the person he is within. How one reacts to the environment is more important than what one can do. Through Wushu I have become a more compassionate, more focused, and more confident person. I hope that what I have gained from Wushu, I can give back by sharing and extending the martial spirit to the world around me.

喀啦！一計重拳，打彎敵人的膝蓋，再一招外擺腿狠狠踢向從天而降的偷襲者，李連杰面不改色地繼續教訓他的對手，碰！碰！碰！三個迴旋腿又讓三個壞蛋趴下，還將他們拋向不同的方向，叫他們疼痛地大叫。

當我四歲時，就喜歡在電視機前模仿中式超人的每一個動作，對我來說，能用高強的功夫打敗敵人的就是英雄。我以為能夠瀟灑地打敗敵人就是功夫的本質與功能。雖然距離那段時光不是很久遠，但我對功夫的想法，有巨大的改變，並且體會了武術對我的意義。

我與功夫結緣始於摔角，四歲開始就去上課。看功夫電影與聽功夫故事，引起我對武術的興趣；加上我對中國文化習俗的愛好，沒有其他的活動，超越我想習武的慾望。很快地，功夫變成我所熱衷的一門藝術，並且珍惜武術訓練帶來的益處。然而伴隨習武的快樂與榮耀，我也不可避免地嚐到武術帶來的挫折與艱辛。

在美國經過三年的武術訓練後，我得到去北京石剎海武術學校暑期進修的機會。我知道這是我一生中難得的機會。出發前的幾個星期，我全心訓練、努力準備，希望在美國播下的種子在中國開花結果。這次的進修對我來說，是代表提升武術技能的機會和拿下更多獎牌進而參加美國代表隊甄選的希望。沒想到就在我滿心歡喜與充滿希望的同時，一次練習的失誤改變了一切，我太過急切的訓練，讓我「跳得愈高、跌得愈重」。當聽到足踝韌帶斷裂的聲音，我震驚地、甚至感覺不到身體的痛苦。我只覺得整個人被失敗與無助全然佔領，心也碎了、夢也碎了。

剛開始，我心中充滿猶豫，不知道應該否取消北京訓練計畫，我不願浪費寶貴的時間與金錢，但因為有父母與師友的鼓勵，我毅然決定捨棄美國舒適的冷氣教室，帶傷飛往酷暑中悶熱的北京，開始一段無法預知結果的旅程。

以某些方面來說，因為受傷造成體能上的限制也有它的一些好處，它讓我有機會從更寬廣的角度來觀察訓練。坐在場邊，使我能集中精神，去觀察同輩與前輩們的訓練。盡管是透過想像，我學到如何專注在假想目標上，不要忘掉動作的實際作用，我同時學到發力點與動作節奏變化的重要。

在我訓練第三周的一個清晨，我一面在武館的鏡前練習舞劍的技巧，一面為自己因為腳傷而力不從心生自己的氣，頹然收起劍跌坐板凳上。突然間，耳聞一陣中國鼓、笛與絃樂串連起來的樂聲。我四處張望尋覓聲音的來處，眼見一個結合速度、集中力、平衡與和諧的太極表演。表演者的每一個流暢與完美的動作，讓人驚嘆不已。那是一種剛與柔完美動作的結合。在音樂結束、表演者離開軟墊後，我在她表演最後一個太極動作的身後，看到兩個中國字—「武魂」。

剎那間，我突然覺悟到，什麼是武術家應該體現的精神與武術的真正涵義。武術並非是讓自己外表看起來很酷、伸展肌肉或打敗對手；它真正的精神是一種透過自我約束對自己的能力負起責任。最重要的是，武術能透過平衡、形式、集中力與堅持，教給人榮譽、正義、紀律與自制力。

英雄並非他只懂得功夫，而是他個人具備的內在素質。一個人如何對不同環境做適當的反應，比他的能力更為重要。從武術訓練當中，我變得更加富有同情心、注意力更加集中與更具自信心。我希望能把我的習武經驗，多與我周圍的人分享。

Charles Shao Hwang 黃孝傳

Personal Reflections 個人感言

"The only way to truly progress was to do it for myself, not to be better than someone else."

— *Charles Hwang*

「真正進步的唯一方式是和自己比，而不是爲了比別人更好。」

— 黃孝傳

Date of Birth: March 11,1985
UC Berkeley Medical School
- 2005 U.S. Wushu Team Member
- 2005 Four Gold Medals (Advanced)
  CAL team placed 1st—National Collegiates at UC Davis
- 2004 Four Gold Medals (Intermediate)—National Collegiates at Stanford University

生日：1985年3月11日
柏克萊加大醫學院學生
- 2005年美國國家武術隊隊員
- 2005年戴維斯加大的全美大學競賽高級組四項個人冠軍
- 2004年史丹福大學的全美大學競賽中級組四項冠軍

The excitement and anxiety crept higher with each step I took. A beaming smile stretched across my face as the music grew louder through my headphones. I felt the sad, worried gaze of my parents on my back as I left them behind, but my sights were set on the International Gate bound for Beijing, China. Beyond the gate was my first solitary journey.

As I found my seat on the plane, I immediately began imagining how much my skills would improve over the next two months at the Shi Cha Hai Athletic School in Beijing. I could hardly believe that in a matter of hours, I would be training with the internationally acclaimed Beijing Wushu Team, the same team that the famous Jet Li had trained with during his youth! Throughout the flight, my thoughts drifted towards questions about what I needed to improve on, how I would spend my time there, and who I would meet.

My commitment and desire to excel at Wushu drove me to search for something more, which led me to the option of going to Beijing to further my training. My enthusiasm and dedication paid off, as I was the only foreigner allowed to train with the actual Beijing team.

The trip itself was no vacation. I was placed in a two-person dorm with a thirteen-year-old boy from Japan who was there to practice ping-pong. Although we spoke different languages, we managed to slowly understand each other through hand gestures and a great deal of patience.

As I met up with the team for my first practice session, I was completely breathless. A wave of aspiration and eagerness to train engulfed me. However, the rigorous workouts of four to six hours a day, six days a week, were more straining physically and mentally than I had realized.

I was ill prepared to train at the same level and intensity of the best athletes in the world. We started with a light, twenty-minute warm-up in well over one hundred-degree heat, at the end of which I was already soaking with sweat and gasping for water. The following twenty minutes of stretching in various splits positions left me teary-eyed with pain. The way the coaches forcefully pushed me down while I stretched squeezed out all my enthusiasm and drive. I floundered through the final hour and twenty minutes of kicking and jumping exercises, forms, and conditioning, with the idea still clear in my mind that I would be expected to do this at least twice a day, six days a week, and for the next two months. Not being able to keep up during the workouts, let alone being able to walk normally near the end of the first week, made me question myself. After the first week,

I worried about being dead weight during the workouts. I began to wonder if I was really up to the test.

Saddened at the fact that I lagged so far behind the youngest members on the team, I felt hopeless and lost, and my determination drowned under a wave of depression. Never before had I faced such a challenge. As I considered the idea of going home and saving money, I found renewed motivation from unlikely sources.

The Beijing Wushu Team members approached me and reminded me that they had spent their entire lives centered on Wushu training. Cao Yue, one of the best at the school, said with a pat on the back, "As Jackie Chan once said, 'I'm not necessarily able to do what Bruce Lee could do, but neither could Bruce do everything I can do.' You are very good considering you've only been training for a year."

This blew my mind. I couldn't expect to be as good as them right away—that was wishing too much. I had to be patient and stop comparing myself to others. The only way to truly progress was to do it for myself, not to be better than someone else. They helped me focus on how to inch one step closer to my goals. Through discipline and patience, I began to rapidly improve after the first week and gain back my confidence.

Back in the U.S., I founded the Martial Arts Club at Los Altos High School. In addition to training with my coach, I work closely with the Stanford Wushu Team. I constantly send pictures and keep in touch with my new Beijing Wushu Team friends. I plan to return to Beijing next summer to discover what new things hold in store for me.

隨著我踏出的每一步，興奮感和焦慮感都不斷在遞增中，當耳機傳來響亮的音樂，我開始綻放出笑容，我感受到身後雙親的傷感和擔憂，但是我的目光集中在通往中國北京的國際機門上。一過機門，即是我的第一次的單獨出旅。

當我找到機位安頓後，馬上開始想像，我的武術技能，在北京石剎海體育學校的兩個月訓練中，將會如何地進步。我很難相信在幾小時之內，我就會與世界級的北京武術隊一起訓練，這就是有名的李連杰年輕時也曾一起訓練的同一個團隊啊！整個行程，我的思緒飄向種種問題，我需要加強那些部分？如何安排時間？會遇到什麼人呢？

我想在武術技能上更上一層樓，終於獲得前往北京進一步受訓的機會；我的決心得到回報，我是唯一得到許可與北京團隊一起訓練的外國人。

這個旅程絕非渡假。我被安置在一個雙人房宿舍，與一名十三歲、來練乒乓的日本男孩暫住一起。雖然我們說著不同語言，卻漸漸能用手勢和極大的耐心去瞭解彼此。

第一次練習武術，剛和北京武術隊見面，讓我興奮不已；那是一種強烈渴望接受訓練的心情。然而，每週六天、每天四至六小時的密集訓練，在生理和心理上，負荷遠超過我的想像。

和世界一流選手一起密集訓練，我在體能與心理上都未完全準備好。在超過華氏一百度的高溫下，我們先以較輕鬆的二十分鐘暖身運動開始，但到最後，我已是滿身大汗而且口渴不已。接下來的二十分鐘，各式各樣的伸展訓練，常叫我痛得涕泗縱橫。在做伸展訓練時，教練使勁地將我的身體往下按，這下子擠掉了我先前所有的熱忱和動力。最後的一小時，我掙扎著撐過二十分鐘的踢腿、跳躍動作、套路等，心理揣測，在接下來的

兩個月，我還必須接受至少每週六天、每天兩次同樣的訓練；我自覺無法跟上大家的腳步，更別說一週快結束時，我是否還能夠正常走路了。這些，讓我開始懷疑自己。第一週過後，我開始擔心自己將成為其他運動員的負擔，我想，自己可能過不了這一關。

更令人沮喪的是，比起同隊中最年輕的隊員，我的程度還是差一大截，我覺得無望和迷惘，原有的決心全消失了。從前我沒有面對過這樣的挑戰，可是當我考慮打道回府、省下這筆訓練費用的時候，我出奇不意地又有了重新開始的動力。

北京武術團的隊員安慰我說，他們和我不同，一生都專注在武術的訓練上；學校中最優秀的選手之一曹越，拍拍我的肩膀說：「就像成龍曾經說過的，『我不見得能夠作到李小龍可以作到的事，但是他也不一定能作到我可以作到的每一件事。』想想看，你才訓練一年，就可以達成這樣的成果，算是很不錯的了。」

對啊，我不能期待馬上像他們一樣好，那是奢望。我必須有耐心，不要再拿自己和別人比較。真正進步的唯一方式是和自己比，而不是為了比別人更好。他們幫助了我，一步一腳印，朝自己的目標邁進。透過鍛鍊和耐性，在第一週後，我開始有了迅速的進步，並且恢復了信心。

回到美國後，我在洛斯阿圖高中成立了武術社團，除了接受教練訓練外，我還與史丹福武術隊密切往來。我經常寄照片到中國，與我在北京武術隊的新朋友們聯絡。我計畫下一個夏天回到北京，再去看看還會有什麼新發現。

of Wushu

第四部
Part IV

**Competitions and
Performances**
競賽與表演

Competitive Wushu
競賽武術

Unlike other martial arts, competitive Wushu is non-contact and non-combative. Competitors execute 50 to 60 highly difficult techniques in merely 1 minute 20 second "taolu," or forms.

Although judging can be subjective, there are "Eight Qualities" which are looked for when athletes compete and perform. These include: hands, eyes, body technique, steps, spirit, breath, strength, and ability.

Forms competition is usually held on a carpeted surface that is at least 26 feet by 36 feet. Each ring usually consists of five judges, with one seated at each corner and one opposite the chief judge. Although competition rules may vary, judging is usually based on a 10-point scale, with 10 being the highest score.

In order to calculate the final score, the lowest and highest scores are often thrown out and the remaining three scores are then averaged. Competitors are then ranked according to their final score.

武術競賽不做身體接觸，也不是用來打鬥的。在短短一分鐘二十秒內的「套路」，選手要完成五十到六十種高難度的動作。

雖然評審可能是主觀的，但有「八項品質」可作為選手比賽和表演時的依歸。這八項包括：手、眼、身法、步、精神、呼吸、力量和技能。

套路比賽通常在至少二十六呎乘三十六呎寬、鋪了地毯的場地實行。每場通常有五位評審，四位分別坐在四個角落，一位坐在主評審的對面。雖然比賽規則可能有所不同，裁判法則通常以十分為基準方式，滿分為十分。

為了較公平計算最後的分數，最高和最低的分數常免去不計，以剩下的三個分數來平均，然後，選手以他們的最後分數來排名。

Major Competitions in the United States
美國地區主要的競賽

U.S. Wushu Team Trials—Baltimore, Maryland
UC Berkeley Chinese Martial Arts Tournament—Berkeley, California
Intercollegiate Wushu Championships—College campuses
U.S. Wushu Union Nationals—Pittsburgh, Pennsylvania
Arnold Martial Arts Festival—Columbus, Ohio
International Kuoshu Tournament–Baltimore, Maryland
Florida Kung Fu Championship—St. Petersburg, Florida
U.S. Capitol Classics International Martial Arts Tournament—Washington, D.C.

美國武術隊選拔賽—馬里蘭州巴爾地摩

柏克萊加州大學中國武術競賽—加州柏克萊

大學武術冠軍賽—各大學校園

美國武術聯盟全美大賽—賓州匹茲堡

阿諾武術節—俄亥俄州哥倫布市

世界國術大賽—馬里蘭州巴爾地摩

佛羅里達功夫冠軍賽—佛羅里達州聖彼得堡

美國華府傳統國際武術競賽—華府

Note: This is by no means a complete list. Locations are subject to change.
註：這不是完整的名單，地點依例也會變更。

The Art of Performing
表演藝術

In addition to competitions, performances are an important aspect of Chinese Wushu. By performing in front of large audiences, students often gain confidence and develop stage presence. Demonstrations typically consist of basics, aerial movements and acrobatics, routines, and occasionally sparring sets. Lively, rhythmic music set in the background often raises the spirit of the crowd.

除了競賽以外，表演也是中國武術中重要的一環。在觀眾面前表演，學生能增加信心，並培養舞台展現的能力。常見的表演包含了基本功、空中飛騰、特技、套路，有時候會有一些打鬥招式。背景中，加上氣勢昂揚的武術音樂，常能激起觀眾的情緒。

Master Tu Jin-Sheng
氣功大師涂金盛

Shaolin Performances
少林寺的表演

In 1999, Abbot Shi Yong Xin of Shaolin Temple in China established three Shaolin performing groups to represent Shaolin Kungfu worldwide. As a result, American audiences witnessed the incredible Kungfu power demonstrated by monks from China's Henan province.

The first show was the Shaolin *Wheel of Life*, which dramatized the legendary story behind the Shaolin Monks. The high-tech, world acclaimed performance combined dance, music, and martial arts to portray the Qing Dynasty burning of the Shaolin Temple. The show was also featured on PBS's *Great Performances*.

The second show, *Shaolin Warriors*, depicted the life cycle in Buddhism by incorporating four scenes of summer, autumn, winter, and spring. The overseas show premiered in over 25 cities throughout the United States.

The third performing group, used strictly for demonstrations, remained near the Shaolin Temple for the purpose of entertaining visiting officials. The group also occasionally traveled to Taiwan or Hong Kong to represent Shaolin.

嵩山少林寺釋永信方丈於1999年創設了三個少林表演團體,在世界各地表演少林功夫,美國觀眾見識了來自中國河南省武僧團的絕佳功夫演出。

第一個表演團是《生命之輪》,將少林寺之傳奇故事戲劇化。這個運用高科技、響遍國際聲譽的表演,結合了舞蹈、音樂和武藝,刻畫出清朝火燒少林寺的歷史。這場表演也在美國公共電視台的《絕佳演出》系列中播出。

第二個表演團是《少林雄風》,融入春夏秋冬四季之景,呈現與描述佛家中的生命輪迴,在美國二十五個城市演出。

第三個表演團,多在少林寺內做表演,示範給來訪的外賓。這一團有時候還代表少林,到台灣或香港做表演。

The state of California declared March 21st as "California Songshan Temple Day" in 2004. Abbot of the China Songshan Shaolin Temple, Venerable Shi Yong Xin, led a group to perform in San Francisco that year.

美國加州州政府於2004年訂3月21日為加州嵩山少林寺日，中國嵩山少林寺方丈釋永信法師率團在舊金山演出。

Sifu Fei Chen
陳飛師父

One of the performers in *Shaolin Warriors* was Fei Chen. He toured with the show in 1999 and 2000, and occasionally performed with the *Wheel of Life*.

Fei Chen began his study of Wushu at a local government-run physical education school since the age of six. As a talented martial artist, he has won numerous awards in several tournaments, including Advanced Weapon Champion in International Kung Fu Championship Tournament, Outstanding Wushu Athlete Award in Shandong Province of China, National Ten Best Star Athlete Award of China, Double Weapons Champion in National Wushu Tournament of China, and Double Broad Sword Champion in Wushu Tournament in Shandong Province of China. He is a sixth-degree black belt.

Fei Chen first went to Shaolin when he was twelve, but he didn't last more than two months. The hardship of training left him feeling out of place, so he returned to his school in Shandong. "I later returned to Shaolin in hopes of getting on one of these official performing groups," he says. "Competition for slots was very demanding. All candidates first had to be selected and trained by a wuseng for several months in preparation. We had to get up every morning at five to jog up the mountain and train, train, train."

Sifu Fei Chen currently teaches Chinese martial arts in the San Francisco Bay Area and hopes to pass down his skills and drama experience to his students.

陳飛是《少林雄風》其中的一個演出者。他在1999年和2000年隨團出國演出，也參加過《生命之輪》的表演。

陳飛在六歲就在山東省的一所體育學校習武，因為深具天分，他在各項競賽中贏得無數獎項，包括國際功夫冠軍賽的高級兵器冠軍。中國山東省的優秀武術運動員獎、中國國家十大明運動員獎、中國國家武術競賽的雙兵器冠軍，以及中國山東省武術競賽的雙刀冠軍。他是黑帶六段的高手。

陳飛十二歲時初到少林寺，但沒有撐過兩個月，艱苦的訓練使他自覺於外，所以回到山東的學校。「我後來再回到少林寺，是希望能被選入這些正式表演團體。」他說：「競爭非常激烈，所有的候選人由一名武僧訓練好幾個月以做準備。我們每天早上五點鐘起床，跑步上山，然後就是不停地訓練、訓練、訓練。」

陳飛現在於舊金山灣區擁有自己的武館，教授中國武術，希望將他的功夫和戲劇藝術的豐富經驗傳授給他的學生。

One Finger and Two Finger Chan
一指禪與二指禪

Monk Shi Hengxiu began studying Two Finger Chan* at the Shaolin Temple at the age of fourteen. Two Finger Chan, which enables Shaolin monks to balance on two fingers, is a highly advanced technique that requires time and patience. If incorrect methods are used, the training can literally destroy the hand.

For Monk Shi Hengxiu, the amazing feat took him seven years to accomplish. He says, "Many people practice for a few months, only to give up in the end." He adds that he differs from others because when practicing, standing on his fingers does not hurt. Practitioners must be capable of directing qi from the abdominal to the hands and must have sturdy fingertips.

Every day when the sun has not yet risen, Monk Shi Hengxiu wakes up to the morning air, which is both refreshing and nourishing for the body. This is a common sight at the Shaolin Temple. Every day the monks begin training from 5 to 7 a.m., and aside from a few breaks, continue to train throughout the rest of the day.

Despite the long and arduous training, Shi Hengxiu hopes to master One Finger Chan in three to four years. "Practicing is a slow and difficult process, but once you learn it you will never lose the ability," he says. "I have the determination, so I believe that I will be able to achieve this feat."

*Chan: A Chinese school of Buddhism that branched from Mahayana Buddhism; similar to Zen Buddhism of Japan. Chan stresses the importance of enlightenment, meditation, and discipline.

2 1歲的釋恆修是河南嵩山少林寺內少數練成二指禪的武僧。他13歲進入少林寺，二年後便開始練二指禪功，經歷了七、八年才修練成功。

二指禪是少林絕技之一，不是很容易練成的武功，用錯方法或是天生軟骨質的人，會將手練壞、練粗、練爛，甚至往後都無法再彎曲；就有人練了大半年，吃了幾年的苦頭，把手指練壞而被迫放棄。「我早就聽說過海登法師有名的一指禪功。到了少林寺後，發現只有一個人在練，而且到世界各國做表演。既然有人練成功，我也想試試，所以就請教我的師父釋延璋。」

釋恆修說，他的師父習武二十多年，對少林寺的每項絕技瞭若指掌，更知道方法，在師父傳授他方法後，他開始勤奮地學習，與別人不一樣的是，他沒有疼痛的感覺。練二指禪必須配合丹田運氣，將氣運到手指，手指到達一定的硬度，才有可能將全身的重量支撐起來。就像練鐵砂掌，有的人練過以後，手會疼得非常厲害，必須用藥去洗、散毒、散氣，才能繼續再練。

但對恆修來說，他因為掌握了正確的方法，從來就不需要用藥去治療雙手。每天清晨天還未亮，他就早起練功，在大地氣場最強的時候，調氣調息。在少林寺內，他與師兄弟通常都是起床後5時至7時上早課，練功二小時，吃完早飯後，8時半至11時半再練功三小時，午休後，從2時至5時，上文課，也練武，文課要點之一就是修佛。

恆修於2001年練成二指禪後，就開始在中國大陸各地做表演，「我在練成時，有兩個師弟在場，我也不知道自己居然會練成功。」他表示，練二指禪進步非常緩慢，但是一旦練成就不會退步。

在少林寺內，有幾萬名俗家弟子，他們專門前往少林寺習武發展自己的事業，寺院內受戒的武僧、文僧約有七、八十位，他們教出的徒弟也繼續待在寺內繼續教學。剛進到少林寺的前二年，恆修感覺「太苦了」，他離開家鄉，思念家人，在寺內天天習武，有時學不好，挨師父揍，棍棒打在身上，挨皮肉之苦，經常渾身痛得無法動彈。

「有時因為太累，練功時，蹲下去就站不起來，到少林寺，每天瘦一、二斤。」恆修說，雖然度日如年，但不斷鼓勵自己，沒有半途而廢，二年後便習慣了少林寺的生活。「許多功力都是逼出來的，不逼，潛能就發揮不出來。」他記得頭一天上訓練課，跑步跑得特別遠，師父引導著往山上跑，在指定的時間內必須上下山。「上山時，我很用勁地去跑，但是下山時，兩腳發軟，根本走不動了」。他拄了枴杖才走下山，後來還因水土不服生了一場病。

恆修的下一步願望是修成一指禪，讓自己成為繼海登大師之後，唯一一指禪功的紀錄保持人，但是否練得成可能還要再等三、四年，恆修說，他有決心，總有一天，必能練成這項少林絕學。

Cheri Haight 薛莉‧海德

"I am a much better person for having gone through the rigors of competitive Wushu life."
— *Cheri Haight*

「經歷了許多激烈的競賽後，讓我成為一個更好的人。」
— 薛莉‧海德

Personal Reflections 個人感言

Date of Birth: November 6,1983
Performer of Cirque du Soleil
• 2003 U.S. Wushu Team Member
• 2002 Women's All-Around Grand Champion—UC Berkeley Chinese Martial Arts Tournament
• 2001 Women's All-Around Grand Champion—U.S. National Championships

生日：1983年11月6日
Cirque du Soleil 演員
• 2003年美國武術隊選手
• 2002年柏克萊武術大賽女子組全能冠軍
• 2001年美國國家冠軍賽女子全能總冠軍

My first tournament experience took place at UC Berkeley in 1997. At the end of the day, my victorious classmates rushed over to me. Excited that they had all placed in their divisions, they asked me, 'Where is your trophy?' I competed as a beginner and hadn't placed. I went back to train, determined as ever.

Winning is not as important as perseverance. Heaven knows that in my competitive career, I've had my high moments and share of disappointments. Wushu has taught me many lessons about competition, human nature, and goal setting. I am a much better person for having gone through the rigors of competitive Wushu life.

To those of you who aspire to compete, I wish you the best of luck. Train often, train hard, and keep your head up.

我參加的第一個比賽經驗，是在1997年的柏克萊加州大學的武術競賽。在一天結束後，在各個分組都拿到名次的朋友們奔向我，非常興奮地問：「妳的獎盃在哪裡？」那次，我參賽初級組，未取得任何名次。之後，我抱定決心，要更加努力去訓練。

獲勝，並不如堅持來得重要。天知道，在我的競賽過程中，我有過高峰，也有過許多的低潮。武術帶給我很多的教訓，瞭解競賽、人性和如何立訂目標。經歷了許多激烈的競賽後，讓我成為一個更好的人。對所有渴望挑戰的人，我祝福你們，多多練習，努力訓練，保持你的毅力勇氣。

Jennifer Haight 珍妮佛・海德

"The true victor is the one who consistently exhibits kindness and sportsmanship."

— *Jennifer Haight*

「真正的勝利者，是持續不斷表現寬大和運動家精神的人。」

— 珍妮佛・海德

Personal Reflections 個人感言

Date of Birth: July 29,1986
Performer of Cirque du Soleil
• 2003 U.S. Wushu Team Member
• 2002 Women's All-Around Grand Champion—UC Berkeley Chinese Martial Arts Tournament

生日：1985年7月29日
Cirque du Soleil 演員
• 2003年美國武術隊選手
• 2002年柏克萊武術大賽女子組全能冠軍

For me, competitions aren't about how many medals or trophies you win. It's about doing your best—keeping your head held high even if you lose. It's not about showing off or getting a 'big head' when one does win or become successful.

I once had a classmate who thought winning was all that mattered. 'That's why they keep score,' he once said. To that I answer, winning is not the only thing that matters in life. The true victor is the one who consistently exhibits kindness and sportsmanship. Some of the best lessons actually came from when I lost.

Good sportsmanship is probably the hardest and most important lesson to learn in Wushu and Kungfu.

對我而言，比賽對於拿到多少獎牌或獎盃並不重要，而是將你自己最好的一面表現出來，即使輸了，也要抬頭挺胸。比賽不是為了勝利後去炫耀或出風頭。

曾經有個一起習武的同學，認為比賽的唯一目的是拿到獎牌。他曾說，那是大家參賽的原因。我認為，求勝不是人生唯一重要的目的。真正的勝利者，是持續不斷表現寬大和運動家精神的人，我有一些最好的學習收穫，實際上來自於失敗的經驗。好的運動家精神是武術與功夫中最難，也是最重要的課程。

Jack Tu 涂聖成

"Accidents can happen, but the most important part is to stand up again and believe in oneself."

— *Jack Tu*

「意外是會發生的，但最重要的是，要再次站起來，而且要繼續相信你自己。」

— 涂聖成

Personal Reflections 個人感言

Date of Birth: Febuary 28,1985
De Anza College, Northern California
• Three Gold Medals and One sliver—2005 The 9th Annual Collegiate Wushu Championships
• Three Gold Medals and All-Around Standing 2nd Adult Contemporary Male—2005 UC Berkeley Chinese Martial Arts Tournament
• Five Gold Medals—2004 Pacific 'Elite' Wushu Kung Fu Championships

生日：1985年2月28日
北加州迪安薩學院學生
• 2005年第九屆大學武術比賽三項金牌、一項銀牌得主
• 2005年柏克萊武術大賽三項金牌得主、成人男子組現代武術全能亞軍
• 2004年太平洋精英武術功夫大賽五項金牌得主

My most memorable experience was the 2003 Canadian National Team Trials. It gave me a feeling of anger, sadness, and disappointment that I had never experienced before. During my long fist form, I pulled my leg in a tornado-split landing. That moment, all I could think was, 'The form must be finished, or else I am finished.'

Even with pain shooting up my leg, I finished the whole form. After the full completion stand, I felt incredibly disappointed. I sluggishly turned my body toward the judges and bowed. All I could feel was numbness from my leg.

I knew that I was doomed, that I would be doomed for the rest of the trials. My tears ran down my face and I fell in front of the judges. I couldn't stand up because I couldn't feel my leg. I tried to crawl, but my dream was shattered. I laid flat on the ground, watching peoples' eyes—their happiness, maybe their considerations. I felt pain, not from my leg but from my heart.

This experience taught me a lesson: accidents can happen, but the most important part is to stand up again and believe in oneself.

我記憶最深的經驗是2003年加拿大國家代表隊選拔賽。它激起我從來沒有過的情緒，包括憤怒、傷心和失望。在長拳套路比賽中，我在做旋風腿時意外扭到腳，那一刻我所想的只是，「無論如何我一定要做完，否則就完蛋了。」

即使腿部的劇痛往上傳，我仍然打完了整個套路，在結束立正後，我感到非常地失望，我遲鈍地轉身向評審們鞠躬，感受到腿上一陣麻木。我知道完了，剩下的所有競賽項目都無法比了，眼淚不自主地流下面頰，我在評審面前倒了下去，絲毫無法站立，因為腿部失去了知覺。

我嘗試要爬行，但沒有力量。我平躺在地上，看著人們的眼神—他們在竊喜？或許是關切？我感到痛楚，不是來自於腿，而是來自於心。

這次經驗教我一課：意外是會發生的，但最重要的是，要再次站起來，而且要繼續相信你自己。

第五部
Part V

Philosophy and Culture
哲學與文化

Chinese Philosophy and the Martial Arts
中國哲學與武學藝術

Philosophical and spiritual components are important in the study of Wushu. As a manifestation of the Chinese culture, Wushu represents the essence of China's long and illustrious history. Chinese martial arts contain elements from three main schools of thought: Confucianism, Daoism, and Buddhism. Confucianism and Daoism are indigenous to China and are considered teachings rather than religions. Many Chinese people also consider Buddha teaching a philosophy.

哲 學和性靈是習武的兩大要素。武術是中國文化的表徵，代表了中國悠久歷史的精華。中國武術包含了三大思想體系：儒家、道家、佛家。儒家和道家是中國本土的產物，一般認為較像是人生觀與哲學，而不是宗教。很多中國人也視佛家教為一種生活哲學。

Confucianism
(Influences most styles)

- Five reciprocal relationships: ruler and subject, father and son, older and younger brother, husband and wife, friend and friend
- mphasizes "li," means courtesy or respect
- High regard for learning and education
- Stresses virtue, righteousness, and improvement of character

儒家
（影響了大多數的招式）

- 五倫，五種相對關係：君臣、父子、兄弟、夫婦、朋友
- 重視禮，禮節教養或彼此尊重
- 極端推崇學習與教育
- 強調美德、正道和修身養性

Confucius 孔子

Daoism
(Influences Taiji, Bagua, and Wudang styles)

- Dao (or tao) literally means "the Way"
- Follow the flow of nature, do not react with force
- Advocates a simple, natural life
- Importance of change

道家
（影響太極、八卦和武當派）

- 道，直譯為 「道路、正途」
- 跟隨自然之流動，不要因勢反應
- 宣揚簡單自然的生活

Damo 達摩

Buddhism
(Influences Shaolin, Fut Gar, Hung Gar, and other Buddhist styles)

- Belief of reincarnation—enlightenment attained through proper conduct and wisdom
- Emphasizes meditation
- Discipline of the mind, life is sacred
- Suffering caused by desire, suffer ceases when desire ceases

佛家
（影響少林、佛家拳、洪拳和其他佛門武功）

- 相信輪迴—經由正確的行為和智慧而達成悟道
- 強調靜思
- 心靈的鍛鍊，生命是神聖的
- 欲望帶來痛苦—無欲則無苦

Buddha 佛祖

Shaolin and Buddhism
少林與佛

Shaolin Kungfu is one of the most ancient and famous martial arts systems in the world. In the United States, the Shaolin Temple Overseas Headquarters in Flushing, New York is the largest and most influential Shaolin temple.

The temple was founded by 34th generation Shaolin monk Shi Guolin in 1995. Previously, he served as the head martial arts instructor at the Songshan Shaolin Temple in China. He also earned the titles "Shaolin Hero" and "Iron Arhat" for his achievements in Chan and the martial arts. Abbot Yong Xin later appointed him as one of the Shaolin Temple's ambassadors to the United States.

Sifu Shi Guolin states, "Personally, I believe Shaolin martial arts have a very close relationship with Damo's Chan Buddhism. According to the Shaolin Temple tome, Chan Quan Yi Ti, the purpose of Shaolin monks learning martial arts is not to achieve the highest martial power. But to achieve a singular unity when you practice martial arts. Your heart and mind cannot be at two places at one time. Your spirit must be very focused, not beyond your boundaries. You can control your body and mind completely. Your spirit, body, and martial arts all combine into one. This is why Shaolin achieved a very unique martial arts system. It is based on Chan."

中華民族數千年的文明孕育了無數的文化瑰寶，燦爛生輝的少林功夫正是人類智慧的結晶。少林武術博大精深，技藝高超，近十年來，透過電影藝術、雜誌媒體的傳播、國際性的表演交流，少林禪武合一的精神漸漸在本地生根發芽，擴大了它在西方世界的影響力。

少林功夫有幾千年的悠久歷史，是中國武術的一顆明珠。紐約少林禪寺總會住持釋果林肩負著宏揚少林傳統文化，結合少林功夫，書畫與禪學，把這項珍貴的文化瑰寶傳揚至西方世界；他希望學生不只習武，更要學禪，達到人類體能與精神的最高境界。

釋果林是中國河南嵩山少林寺方丈釋永信直接傳法者，他說他在美國傳揚的是佛陀教育，是一種哲學思想，並不是一種宗教。「它是超越宗教的，與宗教並沒有衝突。十年多來，紐約少林禪寺總會已有數千名學生，在中西文化交匯方面，有卓著的貢獻。

釋果林字延嗣，是河南嵩山少林寺三十四代傳人，美國少林寺總會住持。他十五歲剃度出家，參禪習武二十餘年，通曉佛法，精通武術，是河南嵩山少林寺住持方丈釋永信的嗣法弟子，有「鐵羅漢」的稱謂。他在釋永信方丈的授意下，於1995年在紐約法拉盛區建立了美國第一所少林禪寺，除了有讓信眾參拜的佛堂之外，緊臨著還有一個禪武堂，讓當地愛好武術者有一處可以學習真功夫的場所。

Sifu Shi Quolin demonstrates "Iron Body"
釋果林師父示範鐵布杉神功

釋果林年幼時體質不佳，因此外公從他八歲開始就教他練明朝傳下來的氣功「五部追終」，透過呼吸調整全身四肢與頭部，也就是以丹田為中心將氣行使至五個末稍，使全身血脈暢行無阻。他從八歲到剃度出家之前，練功從未間斷。

大約在十七、八歲時，有一次，他的師兄弟無意中用棍子打到他，他不覺得有任何疼痛，但棍子卻折段了；他叫師兄弟再用斧頭槌他，他居然絲毫沒有感覺；後來他又請他們用拳腳踢他的胸部、肋骨、背部與腹部，他居然都無疼痛之感，而且越加有精力、氣越足。之後他才體悟已練成外公傳授給他的「五部追終」，實際上就是他一直想練的鐵布杉神功，那一刻，他真是歡喜極了。

在談到氣功時，他說：「很多練氣功的人，是從外到內拍打出來的，但我是從內到外氣調好了，身體就像一個大皮球，有很大的反彈力量。就算不練功，也能保持這種狀態。」釋果林所言不虛，在一次功夫雜誌十周年慶會的公開表演會上，八名大漢抬著粗重的木椿，齊力撞向他的胸腹，他卻立定不動；當他側躺在地上，頭上頂磚，笨重的斧頭從上到下砍向磚頭時，幾十磅的力量將磚頭擊碎，他的頭部卻絲毫未損。對釋果林來說，抱起五百多磅的石頭也是輕而易舉的，對一般人來說，卻是神乎其技。

少林寺的中心思想是「禪拳合一」，釋果林表示，人要健康，必須調和「五事」，外調睡眠、飲食，更要調身、調息、調心，在學習時不必執著任何形式，但要意念專注。他目前正在整理這方面的教材。他強調鍛鍊呼吸的重要性，要學會深呼吸，從內往外展，呼吸有四相，包括風、喘、氣、息、呼吸有聲音，沉重的屬於「風」，長短不均勻的為「喘」，長短均勻可是呼吸比較粗的是「氣」，呼吸均勻、細慢柔長、若有若無者則為「息」；達到「息」的境界，就可讓身體詳和舒展。

Sifu Shi Quolin
釋果林師父

Martial Arts Schools Mottos
武術學校的教規

Through the study of martial arts, students can discover a world beyond the physical attributes of the body. Asides from physical well being, students can develop mentally, emotionally, and morally as a whole.

Most martial arts schools establish their own motto for students to follow. For instance, at the Malee's School of Tai Chi and Kung Fu in Connecticut, students abide by three virtues. These include the Virtue of the Mouth, the Virtue of the Heart, and the Virtue of the Hand.

Virtue of the Mouth: One should be humble and astute. When refining one's body, one should refine one's virtue of the mouth. One should not say one thing and mean another; one should be true to one's word.

Virtue of the Heart: One should be kind, honest, and righteous. One should not harbor evil thoughts. Instead, one should perform good deeds, be honest to friends, and be respectful to teachers and elders.

Virtue of the Hand: One should not use his or her skills to suppress or hurt others. When practicing or studying, one should stop once a point is proven. One should not be heavy with one's hand and should avoid hurting the opponent or partner.

Other major mottos include bravery, diligence, humility, kindness, moral integrity, perseverance, respect, righteousness, sincerity, will, and wisdom.

Jennifer Haight
珍妮佛 · 海德

在學習武術的過程中，學生可以發現一個超越外在體能的世界。除了健身外，學生可以在心智、情緒和道德上得到發展。

大部分的武術學校會建立自己的座右銘讓學生遵守。例如，在康乃迪克州的王瑪麗太極與功夫學校，學生遵從三個美德：口的美德、心的美德和手的美德。

口的美德：
人應該謙遜機敏。在修養身體的時候，一個人應該要同時修養口的美德。不該言不由衷；應該言行一致。

心的美德：
人應該善良、誠實、正義。不該產生惡念。應該行善、誠實交友、尊敬長者和師表。

手的美德：
人不應該將其技巧用於壓迫或傷害他人。不管是練習或學習，在證實自己觀點後即適可而止。不要過度使勁，要避免傷害對手或同伴。

其他主要的教規還包括：勇、勤、謙、仁、德、恆、禮、義、誠、意志和智。

Jennifer Haight and Cheri Haight
海德姊妹

The Salute
武術禮儀

One of the most basic behaviors of Wushu etiquette is the salute, which is often used for competitions, performances, and training. Although there are numerous variations, the most common salute is the Chinese Wushu Association's fist-holding greeting. There are different meanings behind each greeting.

According to Omei Kungfu Academy Master Tony Chen, the fist-holding greeting consists of the right hand clenched in a fist to represent valor and vigor. The left hand is in the form of a palm; the left thumb is bent to represent humility while the other four fingers are stretched to symbolize the four compass points. When the right fist is wrapped in the left palm, the gesture represents the idea that Wushu does not necessarily mean fighting or violence.

武術禮儀最基本的動作之一就是敬禮，常使用在競賽、表演和訓練當中。雖然有很多種類，最常見的敬禮是中國武術協會的握拳禮。每一種不同的敬禮，背後都有不同的含義。

根據峨嵋功夫學院陳朝輝師父解釋，握拳禮是由右手握拳，表示英勇和活力；左手則是張開手掌，左大拇指彎曲表示謙遜，而其他四根手指伸展，象徵羅盤之四方。當右拳被左掌包覆，這個動作代表武術的理念：和平凌駕武力之上。武術，不必然是打鬥或使用暴力。

Hong Dao Wushu Academy
弘道武術學院

Martial Arts Altars
武術祭壇

In traditional Chinese martial arts schools, simple altars are sometimes used to pay respect to deceased ancestors and masters. As a disciplinary gesture, bowing to the altar expresses gratitude for those who have spread martial arts knowledge to future generations.

在中國傳統的武術學校中，有時會有一些簡單的祭壇來紀念過世的祖先和師父。向祭壇鞠躬是一種自律的動作，向傳揚武術技能的前輩表達感念。

Right sign: Respect to ancestors, Respect to Sifu, Respect to teaching

Left sign: Learn kindness, Learn fellowship, Learn Kungfu

Middle sign: The Chinese character for "fire," painted upside down, means "control."

右方文字： 尊祖、尊師、尊教導。
左方文字： 學仁、學義、學功夫。
中間文字： 「火」字倒轉，意謂「自我控制」。

Martial Arts Altar of Wah Lum Kungfu
華林功夫祭壇

Lion Dancing
舞獅

The lion dance is a popular recreation for the Chinese and is usually exhibited during the New Year season. Surprisingly, there are no actual lions native to China, thus the lion dance is a ritualistic tradition based on a Chinese mythological animal. According to legend, the lion dance was developed to combat supernatural forces and has become a symbol of good luck.

The lion head is constructed of paper machê, elaborately decorated wood, and a colorful length of cloth. The color of the lion indicates its age, with multi-colors representing a mature lion and black symbolizing a youthful lion.

Lion dancers must have great endurance and agility to withstand long periods of time. The lead dancer must bring life to the lion by manipulating the mouth, eyes, and ears. Meanwhile, the person controlling the lion's tail often operates from an uncomfortable, low crouched position. The purpose of lion dancing is to imitate the animal's behavior as close as possible.

Kungfu stances and maneuvering play an integral role in the intricate foot patterns of the lion dances, and the performers must have a solid foundation. Lion dancers sometimes balance themselves upon each other's shoulders, which can be two to three persons high. Sifu Thomas Haase of Wah Lum Kung Fu of Tampa, Florida says, "In order for someone to become proficient at lion dancing, it takes many hours of practice over a couple of years."

Lion dances can be performed during any festival or special occasion. For instance, Sifu Thomas Haase is contacted throughout the year to perform for different businesses. "Some businesses want a show for their Grand Opening, while others want a Chinese cultural demonstration," he says. "Some even call us to perform for their wedding."

舞獅是很受歡迎的中國民俗活動，通常是在舊曆年其間表演。中國事實上沒有原生獅子，舞獅是採取自中國神話動物的一種傳統儀典。根據傳說，舞獅的形成是為了抵擋超自然力，而現在已經成為獲取好運氣的象徵。

舞獅的獅頭是由雕塑性紙漿、精緻裝飾的木頭和色彩斑斕的長布料所製成。獅子的色彩表現了牠的年齡，多彩的是成年的獅子，黑色則是象徵年輕的獅子。

舞獅者必須要有很大的耐力和敏捷力，耐得住長時間使力。主舞者必須靠著舞動獅子的口、眼、耳，生氣盎然地表現其神態。同時，控制獅尾的人常得在低彎腰姿勢下操作。舞獅的目的是要維妙維肖地模仿動物的行為與動作。

功夫的姿勢和靈活移動，在舞獅時特別重要，表演者必須要有堅實的武術基礎。舞獅者有時候要平衡站在彼此的肩頭上，有時候達到二到三人高。佛羅里達州華林功夫學校師父唐夏士說：「一個人要精通舞獅，得要經過好幾年、每天好幾小時的練習。」

舞獅可以在任何慶典和特殊場合上表演。例如，唐夏士師父的武館整年都被邀請到各種不同的場合表演。「有些商家想要做開幕表演，有些想要做中國文化的展示。」他說：「有的人甚至請我們在婚禮上做表演。」

Sifu Walter Zuazo 華德・汝艾索師父

"Wanting a goal is difficult but not impossible, because wanting is being able to."

— *Sifu Walter Zuazo*

「想要有一個目標是困難的，但亦非不可能，因為「想要」本身就是一種實行能力。」

— 華德・汝艾索師父

- 2001 Four Gold Medals–Festival of Wushu-Kungfu in Orlando, Florida
- 1998 1st Place–Pan American Tournament in Ontario, Canada
- 1990, 1991, 1994, 1997 South American Champion in Traditional Kungfu

- 2001年佛羅里達州奧蘭多武術功夫節四項金牌得主
- 1998年加拿大安大略泛美競賽第一名
- 1990年、1991年、1994年、1997年南美洲傳統功夫冠軍

My mission is to mold people of all ages and give them the values of Shaolin Kungfu and meditation Qigong—not just the physical aspects of training, but the spiritual and mental development as well. My mission is:

To maintain the mystical aspect of the art

To keep the flame alive in which we must find equilibrium within our bodies

To find harmony with the things in earth and in the heavens

The knowledge to know that mutual help has to be mutual

because everything is reciprocal in this life

Today I teach my disciple, and tomorrow my disciple teaches his disciple. That way, knowledge will become successive like the wind is to the corners of the earth. Wanting a goal is difficult but not impossible, because wanting is being able to.

我的任務是傳授少林功夫和氣功給各年齡層的人，不只是身體方面的訓練，同時還有心靈和心理方面的培養。我的任務是：

承續這門藝術的神奇部份

保持這門火焰，在其中我們必須尋找自己身體內在的平衡

在天堂與人間的所有事物中找尋和諧

這種互助的知識必須也是與他者互助的，因為所有事物，在此生中，都是交互作用的

今天我教授我的學生，明天我的學生會教授他們的學生。這樣一來，知識會像風一樣延續不斷，吹拂世上每一個角落。想要有一個目標是困難的，但亦非不可能，因為「想要」本身就是一種實行能力。

Vara Reese 維拉·瑞絲

Personal Reflections 個人感言

- Studies in the University of North Carolina at Charlotte and New York Film Academy
- Practiced Kungfu for three and a half years at The Peaceful Dragon in Charlotte, NC and three years at Shaolin Temple Overseas Headquarters in Flushing, NY

- 就學北卡羅來那州立大學和紐約影劇學院
- 在北卡羅來那州夏洛特的和平之龍學校學三年半的功夫
- 在紐約州法拉盛少林寺海外總會訓練達三年

"Kungfu is a way of life."

— *Vara Reese*

「功夫是一種生活的方式。」

— 維拉·瑞絲

For me, Kungfu for is not just about training or learning how to fight. It is a way of life. Since I started studying the martial arts, I have become more aware of my surroundings, less stressed, and more open minded.

When I first heard that there was a Shaolin Temple in New York, I thought for sure that I would not be allowed to study there because I was a girl. That wasn't the case. They opened their doors to everyone who wanted to learn. I feel very lucky and honored to have this opportunity, and I cherish it everyday. Kungfu will always be in my heart.

對我來說，功夫不只是鍛鍊或學習如何攻擊防衛。它是一種生活的方式。學習武術後，我開始對周圍環境較為敏銳、壓力減小，而且心胸更開放。

開始聽說在紐約市有個少林寺時，我以為他們不會收女生。其實不然，他們對所有人開放。我覺得非常幸運，而且每天珍惜有這樣的機會。功夫永遠在我心中占重要的地位。

Sifu Jamel Brown 傑梅‧布朗師父

"Through the training of Shaolin, I continue to move closer to understanding my true nature."

— *Sifu Jamel Brown*

「經過少林功夫的訓練，我能更進一步認識自己真正的天性。」

— 傑梅‧布朗師父

Personal Reflections 個人感言

• Performing artist in hip-hop since the 1980s
• Head Instructor of Shaolin Temple Overseas Headquarters' Brooklyn Location

• 自1980年代始的嘻哈表演家
• 少林寺海外總部布魯克林區教練

I feel that Kungfu and dance are similar because they both require a great deal of physical coordination. It takes dedication to achieve refined skills that translate into art forms. There are methods and techniques that the practitioner must understand in order for the art to be appreciated, and it's important to develop a strong sense of eye, hand, and body coordination.

Compared with dance, I feel that Kungfu has a stronger mental foundation and far greater strength, health, and concentration benefits.

Although I've become an instructor in Shaolin Kungfu, I'm still a student. I always aim to gain wisdom by studying Buddhism and applying this philosophy to my daily life. Through the training of Shaolin, I continue to move closer to understanding my true nature.

我覺得功夫和舞蹈是相像的，因為它們兩者都需要極高度的身體協調感，需要專心一致去完成純熟的技巧，以轉換成藝術的形式。練習者必須要瞭解特定的方式和技巧，才能深切體會這門藝術，掌握眼、手和身體協調性是很重要的。

跟舞蹈比較起來，我覺得功夫更能啟動心靈的力量，在健康和集中力方面，也更有助益。雖然我已經成為少林功夫的教練，我仍然視自己為學生。我總是藉由研習佛法而增進智慧，並且在日常的生活中實踐這些哲理。經過少林功夫的訓練，我能更進一步認識自己真正的天性。

第六部
Part VII

The Art of Taiji
太極藝術

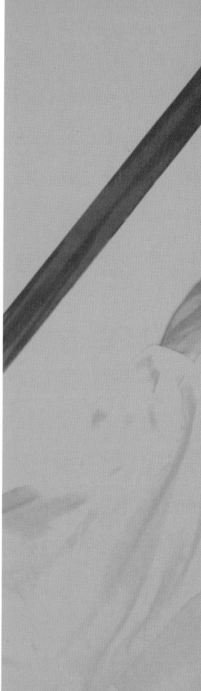

What is Taiji?
何謂太極?

The art of Taiji, which was once a secret among the Chinese community, is now practiced all over the world. Also known as Taijiquan, it is a gentle martial art that facilitates the flow of qi , or "life energy," throughout the body.

Originating from Taoist Philosophy, Taiji is meant to sooth the mind and invigorate the spirit with its physical movements and breathing techniques. The ancient martial art includes both internal and external expressions. By combining mental concentration and graceful postures, practitioners balance the Yin and Yang life force energy.

Although there are several styles of Taiji, the most popular ones are Chen Style, Sun Style, Wu Style, Yang Style, Wu(or Hao) Style, and Zhao Bo Taiji System. Today the 24-step Yang style (a national form developed in 1956) is the most popular form among beginners.

太極拳的藝術,曾經只在中國人之間流傳,現在卻在全世界流行。太極拳是溫和的武術,調整體內的能量。

發源自道家的哲學,太極拳是以動作和呼吸加以配合,來放鬆身心。這項自古流傳的健身方法,講究內外合一,藉由內心的專注和外在的優雅姿勢,平衡體內的陰與陽。

雖然太極有好幾種拳式,最受歡迎的是陳式、孫式、吳式、楊式、武式和趙堡太極拳式。於1956年發展出的楊式24式太極拳,則是初學者最常用的步術。

Grandmaster Dao Yun Chen
陳道雲教練

Benefits of Practicing Taiji
練太極的益處

In recent years, the benefits of Taiji have been widely covered by major newspapers and television stations, such as the *New York Times*, *Washington Post*, *USA Today*, *BBC*, and *CNN*. Media outlets have reported Taiji to be effective in pain and stress relief. For instance, studies sponsored by the National Institute on Aging discovered that Taiji participants (aged 70 or over) took more deliberate steps, increased their walking speed, and experienced a lower rate of falling. In addition, Taiji has been found to reduce stress, improve circulation, and enhance meditation and breathing. Doctors frequently recommend the exercise to reduce stress, improve muscle flexibility, and give an overall sense of well being.

近幾年，美國主要的報紙和電視台都廣泛地報導學太極拳的好處，像《紐約時報》、《華盛頓郵報》、《今日美國》、《英國國家廣播公司》和《美國有線新聞網》。媒體報導太極對於疼痛和壓力的消除有效，例如，由「國家老化研究機構」所贊助的研究發現，七十歲以上打太極的人走路較能自主、行走速度較快、且跌倒率較低，太極能減少壓力、促進循環、增強思考和呼吸。醫生經常建議病患作太極運動來減少壓力、促進肌肉彈性，它能帶給人整體健康的感覺。

Taiji Group Competition at Berkeley Wushu Tournament in 2005
2005年柏克萊武術大賽太極團體組比賽一景

Basic Taiji Terms
基本太極術語

Sifu David Xu
徐德正師父

Qi (chi) 氣
The circulating life energy that is thought to be inherent in all things
生命能量的循環，為所有生物與生俱來的。

Jing 精
Internal energy, essence
內在能量、精華

Pushing hands 推手
Contact drills that are performed between partners
在打拳者之間實行的、碰觸性的操練

Rooting 蹲馬步
Connecting the foot to the ground for balance and stability
足掌接地，將腳與地面相連，以平衡和穩定

Sinking 沈
Relaxing the joints and lowering the center of gravity
氣沈丹田、沈肩垂肘，放鬆所有關節、降低身體的重心

Splitting 引
Taking a force and redirecting it to another direction
將一個力量取來並導至其他方向

Yin and Yang 陰陽
Dao School belief that everything contains opposite forces that are mutually exclusive yet interdependent. Yin qualities are affiliated with darkness and the female, Yang qualities with daylight and the male.
道家的信仰之一，認為所有事物都包含著相對的力量，是互為唯一但獨立的。陰的特質與黑暗和女性相關，而陽的特質則是與日光和男性相關。

Taiji Martial Applications
太極搏擊的運用

In addition to health and spiritual benefits, Taiji can be successfully used for combat. Behind every Taiji movement is a self-defense application, which is the use of a postural advantage to prevent attacks from opponents. Once practitioners increase their speed and learn how to direct their energy, Taiji can be employed as a fighting art.

除了對身心有益處外，太極拳可以成功地運用在搏擊方面。每一個太極動作的背後，都有自我防衛的意義，也就是以不同的姿勢，避開對手的攻擊。一旦學習者學會增加自身的速度與導引其精力，太極拳即可轉換成一項搏擊的藝術。

Sifu Wen Peng (Middle) with Kuan-Nang Huang (Right) and Chi-Sheng Chen (Left) demonstrates Taiji applications.
彭文師父(中)與黃光南(右)、陳志生(左)示範太極搏擊。

Master Shu Dong Li

李書東教練

"I recommend young people who learn wushu to also learn Taiji. Taiji will benefit them in terms of internal energy and spirit."

— *Master Shu Dong Li*

「我建議練武術的年輕人也練太極拳，這對他們在精氣神的表現上，都有很大的助益。」

— 李書東教練

Recognized as a 20th generation Chen Style Taiji Master, Master Shu Dong Li is renowned for his contibutions as a Taiji first class judge, coach, master and record consultant. Today, his name can be found in China's Halls of Fame Dictionary.

Master Li was born in Henan, China and was taken on by the Henan Sanshou team in 1990 to train competitively. Within a year, he captured 2nd place in the Sanshou category and won the championship with free style Taichiquan/sword in a Shaolin Wushu event in Zheng Zhou city.

In 1991, he toured Singapore as both a guest speaker and a performer. After exploring the international arena, he finally settled down in the United States and founded Li's Tai Chi and Kung Fu Academy in 1997.

李書東教練是陳氏太極拳第二十代傳人，國家一級武術裁判、太極拳高級教練、太極專書編輯顧問，他同時被收錄在《中國當代名人錄》中。

李書東出生於中國河南省，1990年在河南省武術散手隊接受訓練，曾在全國武術精英擂台賽中獲團體組第二名，在參加中國鄭州國際少林武術節的比賽中，獲太極拳與劍術冠軍。

1991年，他代表國家到新加坡進行武術講學與表演，開始了國際間的武術教學活動，他於1997年移民來美，並創辦了《加州太極武術中心》。

Sifu Bow Sim Mark

麥寶嬋師父

"Wushu has its own language that can be choreographed into a story; I want to use Wushu Theater to let people know about Wushu."

— *Sifu Bow Sim Mark*

「武術有著它自己的語言，是可以被舞台化的；我想要利用武術劇場，讓人們瞭解武術。」

— 麥寶嬋師父

Sifu Bow Sim Mark is a respected master martial artist residing in Massachusetts. Originally from Canton, China, she founded the Chinese Wushu Research Institute upon immigrating to Boston in 1972, and currently teaches and performs in the area. She is one of the original sources of genuine Chinese wushu instruction in the West. Master Mark is frequently called a "treasure" of either the local arts or the international wushu performing scenes.

Sifu Bow Sim Mark is the fourth generation Wu Dan Sword master. The Wushu Research Institute has published a number of books based on her expert instruction. Her son is martial arts movie star Donnie Yen.

麥寶嬋師父是麻州備受尊敬的武藝家，她於1972年自中國廣東省移民到波士頓，創辦武藝協會，目前在該地區從事教學與表演。她是西方世界中，少數中國武術教學的始祖，在地方與國際武術舞台上被視為瑰寶。

麥寶嬋師父是第四代武當劍大師，武藝協會根據她豐富的教學經驗出版了多種刊物。她的兒子甄子丹是著名的電影演員。

Paul Brennan 保羅·布列南

Taiji practitioner
習太極拳者

"Taiji a wonderful spirit washing therapy
that constantly recreates the practitioner."

— *Paul Brennan*

「太極是一種絕佳的心靈洗滌療法，可以
持續不斷地使人重生。」

— 保羅·布列南

I have been practicing Taiji for well over ten years now. I got into martial arts because I had a hideous temper. I became seduced by the irony that inherently violent people could best be calmed by inherently violent activities.

Martial arts are a model Chan experience: to practice a skill you don't have until you have it, then to practice a skill you have until you master it, then to practice a skill you've mastered until you disappear. I certainly haven't mastered martial arts, yet I feel I disappear a little more each day, and in ceasing to exist I find I exist much more palpably.

I can neither say that I've been cured of my old rage, but I am a vastly different entity than I was before. I find in Taiji a wonderful spirit washing therapy that constantly recreates the practitioner.

我練習太極到現在已經超過整整十年了。我開始接觸武術是因為脾氣不好。我被一種嘲諷的說法吸引：天生暴力的人最好用本質較暴力的活動來平息。

武術是一種經驗禪的方式：去練習一種原本不會的技術，直到學會後，然後去練習該技術，以致於精通它之後；再練習此精通的技術，直到達到無我的境界。我當然還沒有精通武術，但我已經感覺自己每天在一點一滴地消失當中，在學習讓自己無我的過程中，我發現活得更清明。

我不能說自己的壞脾氣已經全部被改掉了，但我感覺自己與過去已截然不同。我發現太極是一種絕佳的心靈洗滌療法，可以持續不斷地使人重生。

Joy of Wushu

第七部
Part VII

The Power of Sanshou
散手的威力

What is Sanshou?
何謂散手?

The word Sanshou or Sanda translates as "unbound hand" and refers to free fighting where the rules are designed to most accurately simulate actual combat. Sanshou matches are fought on a raised platform called the leitai. Historically, the leitai dates back centuries in China where challenge matches were fought both bare handed and also with weapons with no rules. These matches often resulted in death or serious injury. At the National Chinese tournament in Nanking in 1928, the fights on the leitai were so brutal that the final 12 contestants were not permitted to fight for fear of killing off some of the great masters of the time. So changes were clearly needed!

Modern Sanshou developed into a sport about the same time as modern Wushu during the 1960's. In order to define a standard fighting style, great masters from all over China were given the task of organizing the huge heritage of Chinese martial arts into a system of rules in which different styles could complete. Protective equipment was also added to further reduce the risk of serious injury.

散手又稱為散打,直譯為「不受限制的手」,指自由搏擊,規則的設計是依照最實際的打擊模擬而成。散手互打者站在稱為擂台的高台上打鬥。擂台的歷史可追溯至數百年前的中國,當時的對打者在沒有規則的情況下,赤手空拳或用兵器打鬥。這些比鬥常常造成死亡和重傷。1928年在南京的中國國家競賽中,擂台上的比鬥極為血腥,以致於他們不准最後十二個選手出場比賽,以免造成更多當年優秀的大師死亡。因此顯而易見,改變是必要的!

與現代武術一樣,現代散手大約在1960年代發展成一種運動。為了訂定標準的打鬥模式,來自中國各地的優秀大師整理了一套規則系統,其中,不同武式亦能比賽。也增加了保護設施,進一步降低重傷的危險。

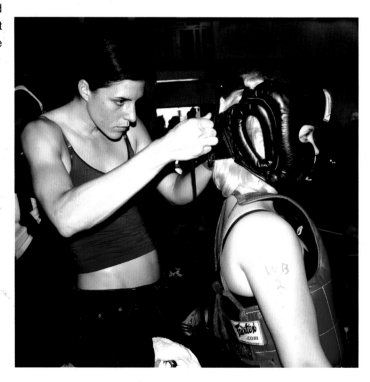

Brent Hamby practices Sanshou with his student Russ Middleton
布安特教練與他的學生米多頓進行散手練習

The Rules of Sanshou
散手的規則

The rules of Sanshou allow for a wide array of full contact punching, kicking, takedowns, and throws derived from the traditional application of Chinese martial arts. Finishing holds (e.g. chokes, arm locks) have been excluded from the rules. Instead, Sanshou addresses the three ranges of fighting—kicking, punching, and grappling. These rules add great realism and fast-paced action to the sport.

A fighter can win by a knockout or by points. In a tournament, opponents fight for two rounds of two minutes each, plus a third round in case the first two score even.

散手的規則讓傳統中國武術的各種應用打法得到廣泛的發揮,包括:全身接觸型擊打、踢腿、摔倒和拋擲,呃喉、鎖臂則被去除在規則外。相反的,散手表達了三個打擊的範圍—踢、打、抓。這些規則強調現場真實性和速度。

比賽者可以靠著一全擊或分數累計獲勝。在一場競賽中,兩對手各比賽二到三回合,每次兩分鐘,兩方分數相同時,再比第三回合。

Coach Cung Le

李康教練

"I don't train just to maintain. I always train at a higher level; that's what has helped me to grow and improve."

– *Coach Cung Le*

「我在訓練時，總是全力以赴，目的不光是保持現有的實力，而是在既有的基礎上，繼續成長與進步。」

── 李康教練

Born in South Vietnam, Cung Le is America's first professional Sanshou fighter and the driving force behind the sport in the US. A world-class fighter, martial artist, and three-time world champion, Cung Le has made an enormous impact on martial arts.

Le has defeated some of the most talented opponents in the world, including Japanese champion Manaro Taro and a Chinese fighter nicknamed "Mongolian King." Le has used his signature move, the scissors kick, in order to beat opponents in competition.

Le has appeared on the covers of renowned martial arts publications, including *Black Belt Magazine*, *Inside Kung Fu*, and *ESPN the magazine*. In 2004, he was also the featured guest for The Discovery Channel documentary "*On the Inside: Martial Arts.*"

At the renowned Asia Entertainment awards in 2004, Le was honored as the most famous Vietnamese Martial Artist in the world; he now possesses over 35 major awards. He was also declared "Sanshou Kung Fu's Top Fighter" in *Black Belt Magazine*.

在越南出生的李康，是美國最早的職業散打手，並且是美國散打運動的推手。他是一位世界級的散打王、武藝家與三屆世界冠軍，對武藝界具有很大的影響力。他受歡迎的程度，使功夫散手受到主流的重視。

李康打敗過一些世界上最佳的散打對手，包括日本散打冠軍Manaro Taro與中國有《蒙古王》稱號的選手。李康著名的剪腿動作，是他在比賽中致勝的關鍵。

李康是許多世界著名雜誌的封面人物，包括《黑帶雜誌》、《功夫情報》、《ESPN》與 《DirecTV》雜誌等。他於2004年在Discovery電視頻道的「武藝情報」紀錄片中接受專訪，也曾在2004年，在著名的亞洲娛樂獎中，獲得《世界最著名的越裔武藝家》的榮銜，目前獲得的獎項已超過35項。

Coach Brent Hamby

布安特・漢比教練

Brent Hamby practices Sanshou with his student Russ Middleton
布安特教練與他的學生米多頓進行散手練習

"Sanshou training is the one constant in my life."
– Coach Brent Hamby

「散手的訓練是我生活的一部分。」
—— 布蘭特・漢比教練

Coach Brent Hamby lives and teaches in Oakland, California. Brent began his martial arts training over 25 years ago. He teaches Taiji, Hsing I, Qigong, Meditation and Northern Shaolin Kungfu and currently competes in, and teaches Sanshou full-contact fighting. He is a three time Sanshou Champion and the 1999 U.S.A.W.K.F. NATIONAL SANSHOU CHAMPION. Brent single-handedly started the Oakland Sanshou Team which has become one of the top Sanshou teams in the U.S. Brent is a current coach for the USAWKF Sanshou Team as well.

According to Coach Brent Hamby, Sanshou training is trul truly great for kids. Not only is it beneficial in terms of fitness, but it is realistic for self-defense and builds a lot of confidence. "I do not think, however, that kids should do excessive amounts of sparring with head contact. Sanshou should always be practiced with proper safety equipment."

布安特・漢比教練在加州奧克蘭居住與教學，二十五年前就接受各種武藝的訓練，現階段教授太極、形意拳、氣功、靜坐與北少林功夫，並且教散手，也參與比賽。他曾獲得三屆散手冠軍，並且獲得美國武術功夫聯盟全國散手比賽冠軍。他成立的奧克蘭散手隊，現在是全美最優秀的散手隊之一。漢比教練現在擔任美國武術功夫聯盟散手隊教練。

據漢比教練所說，散手訓練對小孩非常好。它不只有助於健身，而且對於自我防衛有具體的幫助，又可建立自信。不過漢比教練認為，孩童不應該做過多的接觸頭部的攻擊。散手運動應該永遠在正確的安全設備下進行。

第八部
Part VIII

The Wonder of Qigong
神奇的氣功

What is Qigong?
何謂氣功?

Qigong (pronounced CHEE-GONG) is a collective term for a set of exercises that manipulate the form of qi, or vital life energy. Practiced by millions of people per day, Qigong literally means "energy practice." Qigong is a self-healing art that manipulates the flow of qi through a combination of meditation, visualization, breathing, and movement.

According to Chinese philosophy, qi flows continuously throughout the body. When the flow is irregular or disrupted due to physical injury or mental tension, this causes an imbalance in the system. Qigong students therefore strive to maintain a harmonious flow of qi for the purposes of promoting health.

The ancient art can be divided into soft Qigong (health purposes) and hard Qigong (martial arts and strength training). Practiced in the past by monks, intellectuals, scholars, and ordinary people, Qigong serves martial, medical, and meditative purposes.

For medical purpose, medical Qigong involves a mixture of qi exercises and meditation. The exercises bring about a state of tranquility, thus driving away anxiety and distress. By gaining control of the body and developing positive thinking, practitioners stimulate circulation of blood and qi.

氣功是一種操練氣的方法，氣又稱為重要的生命能量。每天有上百萬的人練習氣功，它能自我治療，藉由靜坐、冥想、呼吸和動作的組合，以掌握氣的流通。

根據中國哲學，氣會持續地在身體中流動。當受傷或心理緊張而變得不規則或被中斷時，就會造成系統失衡。所以達成氣的和諧，可促進身體健康。

這門古老的藝術可以分成軟氣功(健康目的)和硬氣功(武術和力量訓練)。在古時候，和尚、知識分子和一般人都會練氣功，氣功廣泛運用在武術、醫術和靜坐上。

以醫療目的而言，醫學氣功結合了氣的練習和冥想。這練習會帶來寧靜的境界，驅走焦慮，並減輕壓力。藉由控制身體、培養正面思考，練習氣功者可以刺激血液循環和氣的流動。

Thomas Chi
遲佑吉

Shaolin Monks demonstrate Qigong
少林寺武僧團表演硬氣功

Hard Qigong
硬氣功

The original purpose of hard Qigong was to withstand severe blows and attacks from traditional Chinese weapons. Although hard Qigong no longer serves this purpose, today we can see touring Shaolin Monks performing amazing feats. On two separate performances, a monk stood to rest his body on the tips of five spears pressing into his chest and abdomen. Another monk, Zhang Lipeng pushed a car with spears against his throat.

硬氣功最早的目的是抵擋傳統兵器的重大擊打。雖然它不再是為此功能，現在仍可以看到少林武僧表演驚人的硬氣功。在兩個不同的表演中，一名武僧以胸腔和腹部頂著五支長矛槍，另一名武僧張立鵬表演「金槍鎖喉」，用槍頂喉，將一部幾千磅重的車輛往前推進。

Zhang Lipeng demonstrates Hard Qigong
張立鵬表演「金槍鎖喉」

Painting While Standing on Eggshells
蛋上書畫

Qigong Master Tu Jin-Sheng can paint a traditional Chinese watercolor while balancing on top a dozen eggs. He can chop a thick steel pipe with his bare hand, hammer nails through wood with the back of his fist, and to finish it off, immediately play the gu zhen, a traditional Chinese stringed instrument.

Master Tu is a past fighting champion and talented painter and musician. He has written many health related books and has produced several Qigong instructional videos. He explains, "Standing on top of eggs requires still Qigong and light Qigong skills. The purpose of Qigong is to achieve a state of calmness in a very short period of time. The ultimate goal of any Qigong master or method is to control your heart and mind. Any kind of Qigong method should be able to control your mental state and your pulse."

氣功大師涂金盛可以平衡地站在一打雞蛋上，進行傳統水墨畫。他可以徒手劈開粗鋼管、空拳將釘子釘入木頭後，接著馬上靜下心來彈奏古箏。

涂大師是拳術冠軍，一位很有天分的畫家和音樂家。他寫了很多關於健康養生的書，也製作了許多氣功教學錄影帶。他解釋說：「站在生雞蛋上，需要氣功和輕功的技巧。氣功的目的，是在極短的時間內，達到心中的平靜。任何氣功大師和氣功方法的終極目標，是控制身心。任何一種氣功方法，都能練成控制你的心理狀態和脈搏跳動。」

Iron Head
鐵頭功

At the 10 Year Anniversary celebration of *Kungfu Qigong Magazine* in 2002, Master Jack Fu and Master H.B. Chang from China performed an amazing demonstration of hard Qigong: Iron Head. Lying on the ground, Master Fu faced sideways and rested his head on top of three bricks. Three additional bricks were then stacked atop his head. Master Chang then struck downward with a sledge, breaking the top three bricks.

The crowd gasped, but Master Fu stood up without a trace of blood. The physics of this operation are extremely complex, says Master Fu, who has been training for Iron Head for years. There are certain procedures of this kind of training to avoid injury. It is actually very feasible once you have the proper training.

2002年，在《功夫氣功雜誌》的十週年慶會上，來自中國的付學理和張漢斌大師表演了驚人的鐵頭功。付學理躺在地上，臉部朝向一邊，他將頭部靠在三塊磚頭上，另外還有三塊磚頭疊在他的頭部上方。緊接著，張漢斌舉著斧頭，自上而下，一口氣劈開頭部上方的三塊磚頭。

觀眾屏氣凝神，未幾，付學理站了起來，抖掉身上的碎磚，頭上未見任何血跡。這項表演的物理原理極端地複雜，付學理已經鍛鍊數年之久，他說在這一類的訓練中，有一些防止受傷的方法；事實上，只要經過正確的訓練，其實並不難練成。

Sifu Eric Bernsdorf 艾瑞克・伯恩斯多夫師父

"Iron Palm is very arduous training; a lot of sacrifices are made to accommodate the time that goes into it."

— *Sifu Eric Bernsdorf*

「鐵砂掌是一種非常費力的鍛鍊，需要投入很多的時間與必要的犧牲。」

— 艾瑞克・伯恩斯多夫師父

Personal Reflections 個人感言

- Owner of Wah Lum Kung Fu & Tai Chi of U.S.A.—Denver, Colorado
- Performed at the Shaolin Temple in China, Universal Studios in Orlando, Carnival Cruise Ships
- Competed in Iron Palm, weapons, hand forms, sparring, Taiji, push hands

- 科羅拉多州丹佛市的美國華林功夫和太極武館負責人
- 曾在中國少林寺、奧蘭多環球影城、嘉年華遊輪做功夫演出
- 曾以鐵砂掌、兵器、手式、拳式、太極、推手參加競賽

Becoming a Sifu is a long and very tough road. One goes through what we call 'Professional Training.' It consists of training four to six hours a day, six days a week. Waking up at 4:30 a.m. every morning, I would train for approximately two to three hours, then take a shower and go off to work. I would work anywhere from nine to twelve hours then return to training for another two to three hours. Then I'd repeat the process: take another shower, go to sleep, then get up and do it again. I spent three years completing my professional training. After those three years, Grandmaster Pui Chan tested us on the basics and curriculum for four days.

I was not required to break bricks for my Sifu test. I did, however, study Iron Palm as a separate training curriculum. I learned Iron Palm from Grandmaster Chan and trained twice a day for six months. At the end of the six months, I tested by breaking three concrete bricks with pennies as spacers.

Iron Palm is very arduous training; a lot of sacrifices are made to accommodate the time that goes into it. Also, it's important to continue training to maintain conditioning. I have been training in Iron Palm for almost seven years now, and have managed to break five bricks at a time.

成為一名師父，是長遠而艱苦的一條路，要經過一週六天、每天四到六小時的專業訓練。我每天凌晨在四點半起床，先訓練個二到三小時候，沖個澡再去工作。我在工作九到十二個小時後，再回去訓練二到三小時。然後，再重複這個過程：再沖個澡、睡覺，然後起床再重複一次。我花了三年的時間完成我的專業訓練。三年後，陳培大師以四天的時間，測試我們的基本功和所學的課程。

要成為師父，並不需要有劈磚的能力。不過，我還是將鐵砂掌作為自己的訓練課程。我曾跟隨陳大師學習鐵砂掌，每天兩次，持續練習了六個月。在六個月後，我劈開了用一分錢幣彼此分隔的三塊水泥磚。

鐵砂掌是一種非常費力的鍛鍊，需要投入很多的時間與必要的犧牲。而且，為了保持最佳的狀況，持續練習是很重要的。我練習鐵砂掌快七年了，已經可以做到一次劈開五塊磚頭。

Sifu Bob Rosen 巴伯 · 羅森師父

"Iron Palm training helps develop strong focused strikes, conditions the mind and body to work in unison."

— *Sifu Bob Rosen*

「鐵砂掌的訓練可以培養強有力的打擊力、使身心合一。」

— 巴伯 · 羅森師父

Personal Reflections 個人感言

- 1994 Gold Medal in the Open Weapons division—Beijing International Tournament in China
- Owner of Wah Lum Kung Fu of Boston
- Chief Instructor of the Wah Lum Kungfu Athletic Association

- 1994年中國北京國際競賽—開放兵器組金牌得主
- 波士頓中國城華林功夫武館負責人
- 華林功夫運動協會的總教練

In 1979, as I began my Wah Lum Iron Palm training, I recalled my fascination with the breaking demonstrations I had seen in my earlier years of martial art studies. I was curious to find out how these people could break boards, stacks of cement slabs, and red bricks without damaging themselves. At the same time, these were exciting stunts to watch: where else could you see someone do this kind of damage with just their bare hand? So I became an Iron Palm practitioner to research how to achieve these skills and to one day pass on this aspect of the Wah Lum system.

Iron Palm training helps develop strong focused strikes, conditions the mind and body to work in unison, strengthens stances, and allows one to challenge the limits of the human body. Eventually all of this training makes the body a more efficient weapon. The training allows a person to defend against blows as well as deliver incredibly powerful strikes to a target. Herbology and massage therapy supplement the training to prevent injuries.

Wah Lum Iron Palm training is not for every student in the system. It takes a lot of commitment on a student's part to complete the required training. Many Kungfu schools measure this level of commitment differently. Within the Wah Lum system, students must have a minimum of three years of basic training before they can begin learning Iron Palm.

This time requirement allows a student to develop an understanding of the principles of the Wah Lum system's fundamentals, as well as what commitment to training is all about.

Once a student has fulfilled this time requirement, the Wah Lum basic Iron Palm training involves 100 straight days of practice, twice a day. The student needs a private tranquil place to train in the morning and evening. Basic training consists of striking one's hand on a leather or canvas bag filled with BBs, sand, or small stones. The main conditioning surfaces of the hand are the palm, backhand and knife-edge. A student will start with 30 repetitions on each striking surface and build up to 300 repetitions during the hundred-day training period. At the end of the 100 days, the student tests his training by breaking a cement block.

Other training procedures are also important. These include specific stretching exercises to loosen the waist, arm joints, and muscles for a smooth striking motion. Breathing exercises are used to circulate internal energy and relax the mind and body in order to endure the hours of repetitive impact training. Before and after each training session herbal medicine is massaged into the hands. This helps improve blood circulation, strengthen the bones, tone the ligaments and muscles, prevent internal injuries, and reduce the formation of calluses.

1979年，當我開始練華林鐵砂掌時，我想起早年學習武術，曾看到的令人嚮往的掌劈表演，我很好奇如何在自己不受傷的情況下，劈開木板、整疊水泥版和一堆紅磚。這些真是看起來令人興奮的特技；還有那裡可以讓你看到一個人徒手能使出這樣的威力？所以我決心學鐵砂掌，研究著如何獲取這些技巧，有一天再將華林功夫系統中的這項功夫承傳下去。

鐵砂掌的訓練可以培養強有力的打擊力、使身心合一、站立堅實、挑戰人類身體的極限，這些訓練終將使身體化為一個更有效的武器。它能抵擋重擊，對特定目標能使出無可置信的爆發力，而草藥學和按摩可以輔助訓練過程，避免受傷。

華林鐵砂掌功不見得適合所有的人，它需要相當大的決心去完成所有的訓練，很多功夫學校在這方面的要求有所不同。在華林功夫系統中，學員必須至少經過三年的基本訓練，才能開始學習鐵砂掌。

這段期間可以讓學員瞭解華林功夫系統的基礎要領，以及對未來訓練的自備條件。

一旦學員完成基礎訓練，就可以開始華林鐵砂掌連續一百天、每天訓練兩次的練習。學員需要有一個安靜地點，早晚各練一次。基本訓練包含徒手擊打裝滿BB彈、砂、或小石子的皮革或帆布袋。主要加強的部位是手、掌、手背、和掌緣。學員開始是以三十次的反覆擊打，然後在這一百天的訓練過程中，逐次增加到最後的三百次。在一百天過後，學員必須擊破一塊水泥磚來測試訓練成果。

其他訓練程序也很重要，包括特殊的伸展運動去放鬆手腕、手臂關節和肌肉，以達成平順的打擊動作；呼吸練習則是為了強化循環、放鬆身心，這樣才能承受數小時重複性的重擊訓練。在每一次訓練段落前後，需用草藥按摩雙手，這樣能幫助血液循環，讓筋骨強韌、調養韌帶和肌肉，以預防內傷、手繭的形成。

139

Joy
of Wushu

References
參考資料

Books and Magazines

Kung Fu Elements. Shou-yu Liang and Wen-Ching Wu. 2001. The Way of the Dragon Publishing.

Kung Fu Tai Chi Magazine

Martial Arts For Dummies. Jennifer Lawler. 2003. Wiley Publishing, Inc.

The Base of Chinese Wushu. Zhong Yong Jian. 1982. Teck Lee Book Store.

The Complete Boko of Tai Chi. Stewart McFarlane. 1997. DK Publishing Inc.

The Tai Chi Directory. Kim Davies. 2004. The Ivy Press Limited.

The Ultimate Martial Arts Q & A Book. John Corcoran and John Graden. 2001. Contemporary Books.

Credits

P. III: Calligraphy by Au Ho-Nien 歐豪年
P. 17: Photo Courtesy by Kungfu Taichi Magazine 功夫氣功雜誌
P. 31: Story Adapted from Wah Lum Kungfu 華林功夫
P. 38: Photo Courtesy by Dao Yun Chen 陳道雲
P. 39: Illustration by Jessica Liu 劉玉寧
P. 41: Graphic designed by Scott Brookshire 史考特·布魯克夏爾
P. 91: Confucius painted by Dao Zi Wu 唐代畫家吳道子
P. 91: Damo painted by J.S. Chung 鍾正山
P. 106, 128: Calligraphy by Dr. Hsing Kung 龔行憲博士
P. 110, 111: Photo Courtesy by Wen Peng 彭文
P. 116: Information Courtesy by Brent Hamby 布安特·漢比

Useful Websites

America Wu Shu Society
www.wusociety.com/index.php

Combat Application of Tai Chi Chuan
www.shaolin-wahnam.org/taichicom.html

Cung Le
www.cungle.com

EBM Kung Fu Academy
www.kungfu.net/index.html

Hong Dao Wushu
www.hongdaowushu.com

Kungfu Magazine
www.kungfumagazine.com

Li's Tai Chi & Kung Fu Academy
www.tckf.com

Mimi Chan
www.wahlum.com/mimi_chan/

Omei Kung Fu
www.usaomei.com

Ottawa Chinese Martial Arts
www.geocities.com/ottawakungfu

Qigong Association of America
www.qi.org

Raffi's Wushu Wu Lin
www.beijingwushuteam.com

Shaolin Overseas
www.shaolin-overseas.org

Stanford Wushu
www.stanford.edu/group/wushu/

The United States of America Wushu-Kungfu Federation, Inc.
www.usawkf.org

USA Kung Fu Studio
www.usakungfustudio.com

Wah Lum Pai Northern Praying Mantis Kung Fu
www.wahlum.com

Wushu Central
www.wushucentral.com

Wushu West
www.wushuwest.com